ADVANCE PRAISE FOR

BRILLIANT

"*Brilliant* is filled with the knowledge and tools to help people reach their peak leadership performance. It is a refreshing approach to empowering yourself to be both successful and fulfilled, even in high-pressure roles. A must-read for executives."

—**Russell Stokes,** CEO, GE Power Portfolio

"This book is full of insights and inspiration and is an invitation to continue to lean in. It is a reminder to create and hear those positive feedback loops that create lasting change in your life."

—**Teresa Corral,** Partner, Phelan Development Company

"In *Brilliant*, author Jamie Shapiro captures the executive experience. I felt like she was talking directly to me; it just hit home. Our approach to leadership is as important as the solution itself. The answer is within—we just need to learn how to uncover it. Jamie is an expert guide on our journey of self-discovery and trusting our own inner brilliance. *Brilliant* not only identifies the issue, it also provides a logical guide with tangible steps and tools to help us shine!"

—**Julie Tschida Brown,** C-Suite leader

"In *Brilliant*, author Jamie Shapiro does a great job bringing together the individual components and framework for leadership excellence. *Brilliant* creates a clear and defined path to becoming a better, more fulfilled leader and person."

—**Steve Krom,** SVP Sales and Marketing, Comcast

BRILLIANT

BE THE LEADER WHO SHINES BRIGHTLY WITHOUT BURNING OUT

JAMIE SHAPIRO

modern wisdom
PRESS

Modern Wisdom Press
Boulder, Colorado, USA
www.modernwisdompress.com

Published 2020

Cover design by Karen Sperry Design
Author's photo courtesy of Nicole Howe Photography

DISCLAIMER

MEDICAL DISCLAIMER

The information in this book is a result of years of practical experience by the author. This information is not intended as a substitute for the advice provided by your physician or other healthcare professional. Do not use the information in this book for diagnosing or treating a health problem or disease, or prescribing medication or other treatment.

This book is dedicated to the incredible leaders I have had the joy to work with. Thank you for trusting me to be a guide in your journey. Your brilliant leadership, growth mindset, and dedication inspire me every day. I am truly grateful.

CONTENTS

Foreword

I am one of the lucky executives to experience the life-changing benefits of Jamie Shapiro's unique and vibrant coaching model you'll learn about in the pages of this truly brilliant book. Jamie's Full Body Leadership (FBL) Model has made me a better leader, a better mother, a better friend, and a more fulfilled human being.

I met Jamie in 2017 when I was the president of a dynamic leadership development firm. I wanted to serve to my ultimate potential, so I hired Jamie to help me be my best self in leading a team of beautiful hearts and minds. I didn't want to let down my team, and my experience working with Jamie ensured I would not. I learned how to elevate my team by elevating the leadership greatness within me.

The Full Body Leadership Model shared within these pages is a beautiful executive coaching model that is inspiring and wickedly practical. Jamie's heart, presence, insight, and deep love for others is the secret ingredient to the power of the FBL Model. The process connected me to my own leadership potential through my personal story. With Jamie as my guide, I identified personal barriers that were shaped from an early age. I had a pattern of working for toxic leaders who completely drained my energy. It was not serving me, and it was impacting my happiness, my leadership effectiveness, and my presence with my family. Our work together fueled my ability to make a conscious choice to break this pattern and learn to excel as a mother and a leader through better nutrition, meditation, mindfulness practice, and naming and breaking barriers in order to sustain my own brilliance. Jamie's process elevated the power within me to find clarity, strength, and courage to make positive change.

I have been truly blessed to serve others across multiple industries from small to mid-size companies to Fortune 500 and 100 companies, as well as coauthoring *Do Big Things* (Wiley, 2017), a framework for teams to achieve results by identifying *how* they work together, which is equally important to *what* they achieve together. Today, I have the honor of serving as the Chief of People and Culture for Truckstop.com, a formidable fast-growth SaaS company digitizing the transportation industry.

Because of my work with Jamie, we've started a full body leadership movement at Truckstop.com. By creating conditions where talent feels connected, fulfilled, and equipped to do their best work, we have elevated humanity in our own workplace. In one year, together we increased our employee engagement score from 60% favorability to 91% by truly loving and caring about our partners and their experience at Truckstop.com. It is really that simple. My CEO gave me a blank canvas to paint a remarkably brilliant culture and we did just that and we know we can be even better. The FBL Model and Jamie's support are major factors in this success and the many successes I know will follow.

This book will elevate your leadership quest and journey in a way that no other model has been able to pull off. You will need to put in the work and then enjoy the endless gifts that come with the commitment.

You deserve this. Dive in and let's change the world!

Victoria Roberts, Chief People and Culture Officer,
Truckstop.com, and coauthor of *Do Big Things*

PART I

The Full Body Leadership Model

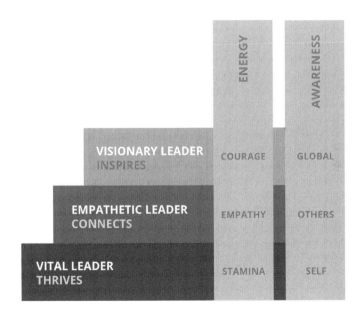

CHAPTER 1

Connecting the Dots of Your Leadership and Wellbeing

Brad wakes up in a fog. He was up too late last night checking emails and putting out the latest fires. He feels groggy and exhausted as he gets out of bed. His wife, Jane, and two girls, Julie and Kayla, who are 10 and 12, are all still asleep. He works for an international company, so conference calls usually start early. This morning he has a call at 6:30 with his partners in Germany. As he drags himself through the motions of getting ready, he wonders if he even got four hours of sleep. He kisses his wife and girls goodbye, being careful not to wake them up. On Brad's drive into work, he starts thinking about his success and his life. He is the president of one of the largest companies in the world. He has worked his entire life to be in his current role. He has financial success and career success, and to everyone around him, he appears to have made it. But Brad feels empty. He rarely gets to spend time with his girls and, when he does, he feels like his head is somewhere else. Just the other day, while sitting on the couch next to Kayla, she asked him where he was. When he said he was right next to her, Kayla looked him in the eyes and said, "Well it sure feels like you are somewhere else with your computer right now." Brad's heart broke in that moment.

Driving to work, he wonders how he got to this place. He sips his coffee, which serves as breakfast on his commute. He questions why his body feels so bad all the time. He recently had blood work done and the doctor gave him a warning to make lifestyle changes. Brad doubts he could possibly make any changes. He has to work this hard. The job demands it and the income he makes supports the lifestyle his family is accustomed to. Jane, Brad's wife, is an amazing third-grade teacher, but unfortunately doesn't make an income that would support the family in the way he does. Brad's mind drifts thinking about his beautiful wife. He and Jane have become distant in the last few years. Raising the kids has become their sole focus when together and he rarely has the time or energy to give to Jane. Brad thinks back to days when he felt a deep connection with Jane and begins missing those moments. As Brad pulls into his reserved parking space in the dark and vacant lot, he feels unhappy, alone, and trapped. With no time to think about things anymore, Brad has to start his busy day with back-to-back meetings and barely any breaks or room to breathe. To make himself feel better, he rationalizes that maybe he will have time to think about making some changes after work.

Does Brad's story sound familiar? If it does, you are not alone. I specialize in coaching high-level executives and while Brad is a made-up person, he is a representation of many clients I have had the opportunity to coach over the years. Brad's story is universal among high-level executives. In fact, parts of my own story are reflected in the story of Brad. I spent much of my career in Corporate America and found myself sacrificing my wellbeing, relationships, and my fulfillment in service of business goals and what I defined then as "success." Unfortunately, we are in a business culture of leadership burnout. Stress-related illnesses are costing organizations in this country $500 million a year. But the real cost is yours. A recent study revealed the most intense jobs in the U.S. in terms of work hours, stress, and physical demands: corporate executive ranks number three, just behind firefighter and surgeon. What is this cycle of driving hard in the name of success really doing for you? Most likely it is hurting your relationships, your health, your happiness, and your overall fulfillment in life. I know it feels like there are no answers and that you are trapped. I am here to tell you that there is a way out of these perceived handcuffs. I am here to show you that linking your leadership to your wellbeing will give you greater access to your leadership potential, while at the same time help your personal life flourish. It is possible. I know this because I have lived it, and I've witnessed countless leaders reclaim their brilliance with the framework I use in my executive coaching business. In the following chapters, you will learn the framework, tools, and processes to tap back into your leadership brilliance.

I built my company and framework from my own experience in the corporate world. As much as I appreciate business and Corporate America, it almost took my entire wellbeing when I was in it. Brad's story is very similar to my own. I spent years in the corporate world going through waves of taking care of myself and then burning out, burning bright and then burning out, over and over again. I had no idea that my health and wellbeing had everything to do with my leadership performance. People were not getting my best in any aspect of my life. Most people were just getting what was left of me, especially the people that mattered most.

I grew up in the business world. My father was an entrepreneur who started a very successful company. I spent part of my summers in his office getting my first lessons in business as a young girl. My first official corporate job was when I was barely 21 years old. I already had my undergraduate degree in business because I completed my last year of high school and first year of college simultaneously. I was thrilled to be in a management position right out of college learning about leadership and business. After working for two years, I decided to head back to graduate school to get a deeper education. I was in graduate school during the first big technology boom and found myself intrigued by the world of technology. While in graduate school, I started to see a gap between the worlds of technology and business that I wanted to fill. I graduated with a Masters in IT and an MBA. During that time, IT and business were two separate worlds and people who spoke both languages were rare. The fact that I could bridge the gap allowed me to professionally advance very early. I spent 16 years in the corporate world in cycles of thriving in leadership positions and then burning out. At the time, I didn't know the deep connection my wellbeing had on my leadership capacity.

I, like most of Corporate America, believed that leadership and wellbeing were two different things. By the age of 25, I had an executive coach and was running an IT division. I was very professionally mature but lacked so many of the emotional tools I needed. I was told in every review I needed more work-life balance and thought, "Great! Where do I sign up for that!?" I wore a pager, had a flip phone, and was on call 24/7. I found myself depleted, exhausted, and lonely. While the executive coaches I had were wonderful, they focused on "between the ears" coaching. They asked me questions around my communication, strategy, and management. What I really needed were questions focused on my emotional health, my horrible travel schedule, my lack of nutrients, and my personal connections outside of work. I needed a coach that was focused on my full body and the lack of care I was showing it. I watched my peer group go through the same struggle. We were getting our lunches from vending machines if we had time, sitting all day, and failing to manage our emotions and stress well.

What I noticed in my career and the career of my peer group was that nutrition was usually the first thing to go. Our schedules got so time-constrained that we often skipped meals, overate from stress when we did have time to eat, and saw little connection between the foods we ate and our leadership capacity. Lack of nutrition led to less energy, which quickly led to giving up our routines around movement. It seemed impossible to make it to the gym, go for that run, or even take time to get some fresh air. Little did I know the importance of movement and brain function. My sedentary and nutritionally deprived lifestyle led me down a path of increased stress, negative reactivity, and exhaustion.

When I left Corporate America, I wanted to change the pattern of leaders being disconnected from their bodies, so I decided to be a new type of bridge in my career that connected the worlds of leadership development and wellbeing. I left the corporate world and went back to school for another two years. This time, I went to get my education in executive coaching and nutrition. Both of my schools were very confused by my education path. They asked, "What are you going to be—a leadership coach or a nutritionist?" When I said both, I got confused looks. This was in 2011, so the worlds of wellbeing and leadership truly had not been brought together. I am happy to report there are numerous companies that now understand this connection and our organization, Connected EC, is dedicated to bringing the worlds of leadership development and wellbeing together to help leaders like you find a new level of performance, personally and professionally.

For years in the business world we have had what I call a "between the ears" model for leadership. Under that model, what mattered most was what was happening in our brains, with very little connection to the impact on our full body. Being a brilliant leader was all about your intellectual capacity. The model and change I want to share with you is redefining brilliant leadership as *Full Body Leadership*. The Full Body Leadership Model (FBL Model) allows you to shine completely in all aspects of your life. Brilliant leadership leverages the intelligence of your mind and body to give you a new view on your leadership, your team's leadership, and your organizational culture. We used to believe that our brains "drove the bus" of our lives, meaning we thought it and therefore we did it or felt it. What we know now from many years of research into social science, hormone monitoring, and brain scans, is that our bodies drive the bus too. Our bodies impact everything from the neurotransmitters that are fired in our brains, to the hormones like adrenaline and testosterone being released in our bodies. Our bodies impact how we think, lead, and connect. If we want to be truly successful and fulfilled, we can no longer talk about leadership without talking about the wellbeing of the whole body.

When I began my journey in connecting the dots between leadership and wellbeing, I searched high and low for leadership models that made the connection. I was disappointed to find they did not exist. I decided to create a model based on what I knew about the corporate world, my experience in leadership coaching, and the existing research and science on leadership and wellbeing. I spent months researching and pulling the data together. It became clear very quickly that there were several elements of leadership that were completely tied to our wellbeing and are critical to the FBL Model. I want to share just a few pieces of research here (and I promise to share more as we go on):

- A key to leadership is cognitive agility—the ability to learn, focus, adapt, and think creatively in constantly changing conditions. Cognitive agility is maximized through proper nutrition and health due to the high requirements of the brain. The brain is a blood-hungry, food-hungry, and oxygen-hungry organ. It requires proper nutrition to be utilized effectively.—*Center for Creative Leadership*

- Fruits and vegetables contain vital nutrients that foster the production of dopamine, a neurotransmitter that plays a key role in the experiences of curiosity, motivation, and engagement. They also provide antioxidants that minimize bodily inflammation, improve memory, and enhance mood.—*Harvard Business Review*

- Various studies have shown that more movement during the day leads to increased energy, engagement, motivation, and intrinsic motivation.—*New Balance's The Organization in MOTION™ study*

- Body posture can change not only our executive presence in other people's view, but more importantly, can change how we see ourselves. Body posture can change testosterone levels, decrease cortisol (our stress hormone), and increase feelings of power and tolerance for risk. Our body posture can also create higher levels of self-esteem, more arousal, better mood, and lower fear.—*Amy Cuddy, social psychologist, professor and researcher at Harvard Business School*

- Emotional Intelligence is the single most important factor in predicting leadership success; twice as important as IQ and technical skills combined. Emotional Intelligence is the capacity to recognize our own feelings, the feelings of others, and our situations effectively. The practice of mindful leadership has been shown as the most effective tool to expand our emotional intelligence and resiliency as leaders.—*Harvard School of Business*

This research, along with many other studies that I will share throughout this book, led to our FBL Model and is the foundation to how I work with clients like Brad. Together we will explore the many levels of leadership and how you can cultivate more energy, more efficiency, and ultimately more satisfaction in your overall work-life balance.

I am sure you have read many books and articles on leadership. Here is my commitment to you: I spend my life working with people just like you and taking them on the journey we will experience in this book. It works. This is not a magic pill or a silver bullet. I will share real tools that you can apply to your life today. You will make small changes that will lead to the next small changes that will lead to the next changes. You will learn how to fit the lessons in this book and the suggested tools into your busy life so that you can break free of your handcuffs and be at your best. Your brilliance will allow you to be at your best in leadership and in life with time and energy for you and everyone you care about. I have lived the busy, non-stop burnout you face. I know the challenges of making positive, sustainable changes. I understand your time constraints. This book highlights the proven process we have used to reignite the brilliance of high-level leaders—it will help you break free of the cycle of burnout one step at a time. I am truly honored and excited to be on this journey with you. My passion and mission in life is to clearly define and share the Full Body Leadership Model to help extraordinary people like you shine brightly without burning out.

CHAPTER 2

The Journey to Building Your Brilliance

In my twenties, I was driving hard in every aspect of my life. I was a competitive triathlete and had to eat well to sustain my thrice-daily training workouts. By 28 years old, I had achieved my goal to be a vice president of a software company before the age of 30. As I moved up the corporate ladder into an executive role, I stopped competing and found myself turning to sugary foods in moments of stress. As the VP of Professional Services for a large software company, I ran the East Coast division of the company and the office in Washington, D.C. A least once a day, I would find myself in one of the many bakeries and ice cream shops near my office in DuPont Circle, where I would treat myself to a cupcake, milkshake, brownie, candy bar, or just about anything with chocolate. My stress levels were off the charts and I was losing myself, my health, and my happiness. I had put on 30 pounds and was feeling sluggish and disconnected from my once-athletic body. My husband, Sam, and I were in the process of trying to get pregnant and I had sadly already had two miscarriages. My stress levels were higher than I had ever felt in my life. I used to pride myself on my calm demeanor and connection with people, but now I often got impatient about performance, leaving people feeling that my expectations were unreasonable and unachievable. I felt ashamed and out of control in my personal and professional life.

It was 7 p.m. on a cold winter day and I had just had another difficult conversation with a customer. The customer was frustrated by the new software release and was yelling at me to get my team to fix the issue tonight. As I hung up the phone and looked around the empty office, I began to cry. My emptiness was overwhelming, and I knew I could no longer sustain this pace or lifestyle. My weekly travel schedule and life in hotels only made things harder. My heart hurt and I missed who I used to be. On my drive home that evening, I decided that something had to change, but I didn't know where to turn for help. I absolutely loved being a leader, but I had completely lost myself in the process. I had become so focused on others' definition of success that I no longer knew what success was for me. I felt lost, unfulfilled, and exhausted. My journey to finding myself again started with a small step. My first step was to tell my husband that I needed help and was no longer happy in the career I had worked so hard to build. That heart-to-heart conversation led me to where I am now and rebuilding my own brilliance through the FBL Model.

This is just a piece of my personal journey and even though it sounds depressing, I truly love Corporate America. I know, you don't hear that very often. The way I see it, Corporate America is a place with incredible potential to help build amazing communities of people with extraordinary leaders who are great contributors to society. However, to do this we need to change how we think about leadership and begin to transform our business communities into true places of wellbeing. Our leaders and the communities they serve should have a foundation of wellbeing. In order to do that, we need to stop thinking about leadership development and corporate wellbeing programs separately. A complete integration where we are focused on wellbeing as the foundation of leadership will give us new levels of performance and organizational health. Business communities are true communities. A hundred years ago, we worked and lived in the same place. We could impact change in those communities more seamlessly. We now spend two-thirds of our waking life at work and yet we are failing to see that these places are true communities that we can positively impact. It is time we recognize that our places of work have the responsibility to care for people in new ways that simultaneously enhance their overall wellbeing and leadership. This starts with our leaders. Leaders are our role models and the people our organizations look up to. We need to start treating leaders with care and attention to their wellbeing. We can, and should, create communities where we shine brightly without burning out.

When we lead our companies from the perspective of the FBL Model, we become role models for how to be at the top and also be a fulfilled, healthy human being. Being that type of role model is what helps move the needle in creating business communities of wellbeing. We can start a movement together that helps to improve the health of our workplaces, our leadership potential, and the wellbeing of our nation. While I don't think the solution for our society is only in our business communities, I do believe we can make a difference when we change our lens in business. As leaders, we are often sharing the importance of employee wellbeing programs while at the same time making excuses why they can't work for us. Let's change this. Let's find a new model that allows us to connect our health to our leadership and help our communities do the same. I believe the FBL Model does that.

The Connected EC FBL Model and The Journey Ahead

In the next chapters, you will learn the framework we use to coach individuals and groups to connect the dots in leadership and well-being to make lasting changes. We specialize in coaching executives, so please know if you are a busy leader with very little time, this book is truly for you. With each chapter, you will take one small step that will lead you to real transformation. This book is meant to be a guide and a toolset for you. I wanted to provide you with the tools I use every day with my clients to help transform their lives. I recommend reading one chapter at a time and giving yourself practice with each chapter before moving on. Each tool I share will be immediately applicable to your life and will not take extensive time or energy to implement; However, it will take practice. Throughout the book I will be sharing my journey and my client Brad's story with you. His story, created for this book, takes place over the course of a year, which is my typical timeframe for working with a client. Please do not rush through the exercises or tools I share with you. My recommendation is to spend at least a week with each chapter, focusing on the tools and concepts within that chapter before moving on. The framework of the FBL Model starts with you and a focus on yourself.

My personal corporate experience and deep research into the art of leadership and the science of wellbeing, paired with extensive client experiences, led to the development of our FBL Model. This model looks at both energy and awareness for you, your relationships, and more globally, your organization and community. We break this into three levels of leadership: Vital Leadership, Empathetic Leadership, and Visionary Leadership. We focus on helping you become brilliant in all aspects of your leadership and life. This book will guide you toward becoming a balanced leader experiencing your highest levels of wellbeing and performance.

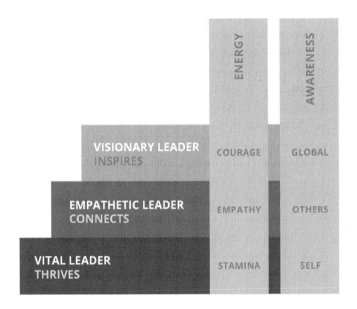

Let's start our journey with the concept of Vital Leadership. Leadership can be seen as a series of building blocks that starts with the foundation of self-awareness. My mother was the first person that truly taught me about leadership. When I was a young woman, making some not-so-great decisions in my love life, my mom sat me down to talk about my struggles. She told me one of the most important lessons in life was that in order to love another person, I first needed to learn to love myself. That lesson is at the foundation of the first level in the model: Vital Leadership. In order to lead others, we first need to lead ourselves. When you have the energy and awareness for self first, you can maximize your leadership and life. Vital leaders shine brightly, rather than burning out, by being mentally, emotionally, and physically agile and resilient. You cannot serve from an empty vessel, and this first level of leadership becomes the foundation for connection with others and visionary leadership.

Mastery of Vital Leadership allows you to accomplish more and keep up with the demands of work and life without burning out.

When I was working long hours in Corporate America like Brad, the concept of work-life balance was elusive and I had no idea how to execute it in my life. We all have 24 hours in the day, and we know time is a limited resource. No matter how hard we try, we cannot add hours to the day. However, energy is a different story. While energy is a limited resource, we do have the ability to replenish and recharge that resource. The first step in connecting the dots of your leadership and wellbeing is to gain a better understanding of your energy.

When I started my company, that was one of my first priorities: to break down what "work-life balance" and "replenishment" really meant. Even before I began my work developing the FBL Model, I knew the understanding of energy in leadership was foundational. I remembered in my ninth-grade physics class my teacher lit a candle and explained that the candle was using energy, and when the energy was gone the candle would burn out. I know as a leader you have a lot of energy going out into the world: energy for your projects, teams, company, family, community, and perhaps boards you sit on, and the list keeps going. But what about energy back in? Brilliant leadership starts with the foundation of energy and stamina. How are you making sure that flame doesn't extinguish? You see, we are all different in our energy needs, and everyone has different things that bring us energy. One person may find their energy by reading a great book, while someone else may need to find time in nature, and another person may be truly replenished by a hot bath in the evening. We all need to discover what replenishes our energy and be intentional about doing some of these things each and every day. Let's break it down, which will allow us to focus on one small thing at a time that refills your energy.

Think about the following four categories of energy usage: 1) body/physical, 2) mind/intellectual, 3) heart/emotional, and 4) spirit. In each category, imagine what gives you energy. It can be something you have done before, something you have never done and want to explore, or things you are doing now. For body, think about the things that serve your physical body, such as taking walks, eating good food, getting quality sleep, or going to the doctor. For the mind, think about the activities that intellectually stimulate you and give you energy at the same time, like reading books, having good conversation, listening to podcasts, etc. For the heart, ask yourself: What fills your heart? Is it relationships, community, giving back, etc.? These are just ideas to get you started. And finally, there is your spirit. People always ask if I am speaking about religion and spirituality in this category, and my answer is always "Maybe." Spirit is anything that connects you to your highest self and to something greater than yourself. For some people that is religion and spirituality. For others, it might be being outdoors or meditation. This is truly an individual experience. Everyone is different. When we universally tell people to find work-life balance, it falls flat because there are so many dimensions to finding balance. There is a worksheet on the next page for you to use in this process, along with an example of a completed one. The completed example you see first shows some of my energy replenishments. Use the blank worksheet to list as many things as you can that give you energy. You can list things that you are currently doing, things you have done in the past, and things you have never tried but you think might give you energy. Don't worry, I am not going to ask you to start doing every activity you list on your worksheet. This will be a page you can use as you read this book. You will come back to this worksheet and write down additional items as you learn them. Spend at least five minutes now writing down as many things that you can think of that give you energy and replenish you. (This worksheet, along with all others in the book, can be downloaded at www.connectedec.com/brilliant-book.)

Energy Worksheet Example

List under each category things that replenish you and give you energy.

Mind/Intellectual	Heart/Emotional
Intellectual conversations with friends Researching—nutrition, wellbeing, positive psychology Reading books and blogs Leadership conferences Listening to podcasts Writing Coaching	Quality time with my spouse Serving on non-profit boards Random acts of kindness Quality time with my kids Extended family time Time with my dog
Body/Physical	**Spirit**
Yoga CrossFit Wakeboarding Meditation Getting good sleep Eating well Snowboarding Walking/hiking with my dog	Prayer Yoga Time in nature Meditation Community-building time Looking at the mountains Connecting deeply with others

Energy Worksheet

List under each category things that replenish you and give you energy.

Mind/Intellectual	Heart/Emotional
Body/Physical	**Spirit**

To download an Energy Worksheet, visit www.connectedec.com/ brilliant-book.

Why start with energy? Energy replenishment is the foundation to expanding into our most powerful leadership potential. Energy is what fuels brilliant leadership and fundamental wellbeing. It is also the first step in understanding the FBL Model. We need to start thinking of ourselves as a valuable resource that can be replenished. However, we need to be intentional about it. We have all been on an airplane when the flight attendant tells us to put on our oxygen mask first before assisting others. I want you to think about this in leadership. We need to lead ourselves first before we can effectively lead others. It truly starts with you.

To be able to consistently meet the challenges of your leadership role, you are required to have stamina: physical, mental, and emotional stamina. As you begin to work on your Vital Leadership through the Energy Worksheet, you will learn to see your energy replenishment through the lens of mind, body, heart, and spirit, which allows you to begin thinking about how to rebuild this valuable resource for your vitality.

Self-awareness at the Vital Leader level involves becoming more responsive and less reactive. We all have patterns of thinking, behaving, and relating that get in the way of our ability to achieve our goals. With Vital Leadership, you will bring more conscious awareness to your emotions and thoughts as well as the deep-seated beliefs and motivations that lie beneath these feelings. Mastery of this level will enable you to be more fully present in all domains of your life—at work, at home, in your community, and with yourself. We will spend the majority of our time together in this book building your Vital Leadership. This level of leadership development is the most overlooked and the foundation to all other aspects of leadership.

The foundation of Vital Leadership, enabled by self-awareness and energy, allows us to easily shift awareness from self to others. You can then utilize your foundational energy and awareness to become a leader with more capacity for others. The second level, Empathetic Leadership, is about cultivating empathy, emotional intelligence, and connection with others. Empathetic leaders are able to connect quickly because they are listening to others with curiosity and openness. When you have the needed energy at this second level, you can create strong emotional connections with others in ways that motivate and deepen understanding. Empathy functions like electricity that connects people. Expanding your capacity to be open, warm, and present will help you connect and create authentic bonds of trust. You can remain aware of your own emotional states, while also tuning into what others are feeling, giving you reliable insights into their thoughts and motivations. Your employees, colleagues, and customers will feel that you care, which generates loyalty, enhances collaboration, and improves performance. Through creating deeper relationships and understanding of others in all aspects of your life, you will be able to grow to the third level of the model, Visionary Leadership.

Visionary Leadership is the category that most leaders want to build first. Time and time again, I hear from clients that they want to expand their abilities to inspire. It is true that visionary leaders inspire people to do great work. They are able to chart innovative and strategic ways forward and communicate their vision so that others want to follow. While this is an essential part of leadership, the foundations have to be there to actually fully expand into this level. You need to have the energy to summon the courage to move into uncharted territory, take an unpopular stand, or navigate organizations through difficult challenges. Courage is not the absence of fear; rather, it is an energy that allows you to act in the face of fear and inspire others to follow.

To lead with courage requires a clear sense of purpose that is authentic to your own values combined with a capacity to communicate your vision and to persevere. The building block at the Visionary Leadership level is global—organizational, at a community level, and beyond. Global awareness gives you the ability to see the big picture from all angles and respond powerfully. It is the ability to sense what is going on with interconnected groups of people—customers, competitors, internal teams—rather than just one or two people. With global awareness, you will be able to develop an innovative and strategic vision for the organization that people can get behind.

The FBL Model is used as our roadmap for building your energy and awareness at each level to achieve your full leadership potential. Each chapter will focus on an important building block to help grow your capacity to lead. Let's begin with the overview of our journey and a summary of each chapter.

Listen to Your Inner Wisdom to Discover Your Vision and Values

Vital Leadership starts with energy for self and self-awareness. The first step in self-awareness is getting connected to your best self and your inner wisdom. When you get grounded and connected to your personal and professional vision, you can make lasting changes that have deep impact. You will learn tools and techniques to help you listen, to connect deeper to your internal wisdom, and to explore your core values as a leader. This is a critical first step to real wellbeing.

Fuel Your Leadership with the Right Food

The world of nutrition and leadership are rarely talked about together, yet food is the foundation of our energy to lead. Don't worry, I am not going to give you a meal plan or tell you to start a rigid diet. However, I will show you how food impacts you both psychologically and physically and how that influences you both personally and professionally. You will learn easy and simple ways to make changes that will transform how you feel and think every day, even with a busy schedule. You will see how good food provides us with the stamina to meet the demands of our lives.

Lead with Your Body to Increase Your Executive Presence

Once we have the foundational energy to meet the physical demands of our day and awareness of our values as a leader, we will see how movement practices can foster even greater connection, confidence, and wellbeing for the mind and body. I will share the science and research around the body's role in driving the bus of our minds and its impact on our leadership. We will explore tools and techniques that you can apply throughout your day that will impact your engagement, creativity, energy, and connections so you can continue to build your Vital Leadership and create the base for developing Empathetic Leadership.

Practice a Positive Mindset to Build Resiliency

Wayne Dyer, an internationally renowned author and speaker in the field of self-development, wrote, "Change the way you look at things and the things you look at change." Our mindset shapes how we handle the day-to-day changes and challenges we face as leaders. Through understanding and awareness, you will start to see how your mind works and how to be more in control of your own thinking. We will explore tools to build a positive mindset and resiliency with real applicable tools. You will grow in your Vital Leadership and enhance your ability to connect with those around you, even in times of pressure, which will expand your Empathetic Leadership.

Raise Your EQ (Emotional Intelligence) Through Mindful Leadership

I know mindfulness has become a buzzword in the corporate world. I will share with you why this trend is here to stay and how neuroscience supports that. Mindful leadership creates more self-awareness and a deeper understanding of others. You will learn to be the master of your own mind and emotions, as well as your responsiveness. The access point to our greatest emotional intelligence and our resiliency as leaders is mindful leadership. I will help you see the small changes you can make that will transform your leadership and connections, making you a true Empathetic Leader.

Break Through Barriers in Your Mind by Working with Your Saboteurs

When it comes to navigating change, the greatest barriers we face are often within our own minds. I will help you through the process of breaking through your own mental limitations and constraints that are holding you back. We will explore the voices that come up during both personal and professional change. You will learn to treat yourself with compassion, while at the same time focusing your energy on the voices that help you excel and grow. Every human being has what we call "saboteur" voices, those internal negative thoughts that limit our greatest potential. Through learning to work with your saboteurs, you will continue to cultivate your Vital Leadership in awareness and expand your Empathetic Leadership at the same time. In this chapter, we will explore and become masters of these thoughts and learn how to work with them, not against them. Making lasting change that sticks long-term takes planning and execution. We will also create a solid plan to help you stay with the changes we explore together throughout this book. Creating intention and a plan will help you make the lasting changes personally and professionally.

Create a Community and Work Culture that Shines

If we want to create the change we want to see in the world, it starts with us. It takes courage and awareness for us to help build our communities into truly supportive places of wellbeing. Finally, we will focus on building your Visionary Leadership and creating cultures of accountability. You will learn to find your tribe and build deeper trust and connection in order to transform your workplace. You will be shining so brightly that you will become the catalyst of change and start a movement that integrates leadership and wellbeing. It is time to begin our journey together!

PART II

Building the Foundation of Vital Leadership

CHAPTER 3

Listening to Your Inner Wisdom to Discover Your Vision and Values

The first time I met Brad was in his office. His office was beautiful with sprawling windows that overlooked the city. I quickly saw the pictures of his family and the personal touches he had on the walls. Brad loved nature and had several artistic photos of the mountains. As I observed his pictures, Brad told me he once was an avid skier and hiker, but that had all changed in the last 10 years. I also noticed several large stacks of paper and files spread around haphazardly. Brad commented that he never had time to organize his desk and asked me to excuse the clutter. We sat down on the couches in his office and he shared with me that he was looking for an executive coach to help him achieve the challenging business goals he had in front of him for the year. He wanted his team to perform at a higher level and be committed to the work in front of them. As we started talking, he also shared his health goals. He wanted to get his health back on track and said if his next physical was better that would be great. Many clients I meet start exactly where Brad started with me: sharing their goals. Goals are fantastic and we will talk more about them later, but they are not the best place to start for lasting change, both personally or professionally. If we want sustainable change in our lives, we need to start by connecting to our vision of what is possible at a much deeper level.

Think about this for a minute: We are in the information age and have more information at our fingertips than we have ever had. We should be able to put a goal out there, figure out how to achieve it and move forward, yet most people don't. Why? Even if we add motivation to the mix, most people will not be able to make the changes they desire. Health is a great example of this. We have more information on how to make significant health changes than we have ever had. There is motivation from our doctors, family, friends, and media constantly. So why is health in this country deteriorating instead of improving? The reason is illuminated through two important studies.

The first study was done by Dr. Edward Miller, the dean of the medical school and CEO of the hospital at Johns Hopkins University. The study Dr. Miller conducted took a sample of patients who had been through heart bypass surgery. They gave these patients everything they would need to make a significant lifestyle change: nutrition information, meal plans, exercise regimes, stress reduction practices, and access to professionals. The motivation was simple: Either make a significant lifestyle change or you might not be on this earth anymore. Unfortunately, they found that on average only one in seven people were able to make a change. What was missing?

Dr. Dean Ornish, out of Berkeley, California, conducted the second study, of a similar sample population: people who had been through heart bypass surgery. Dr. Ornish decided to try to figure out the missing piece. Similar to the Johns Hopkins study, he gave the patients access to all the information and resources they needed, but he did two things differently. The first thing he did was help them connect to a place of possibility and vision instead of fear. He helped each patient envision their lives with total wellbeing and what was possible for them if they achieved a healthy lifestyle. He also created a community of support within the patient group. With these two changes in the study, he found that on average six in eight people were able to make a significant lifestyle change. The biggest difference Dr. Ornish made was coming from a place of possibility versus fear. He also helped these patients connect to their personal vision for their lives.

One way to frame personal vision is to start with your "Why." Simon Sinek, best-selling author and motivational speaker, coined the idea of personal and organizational vision as a "Why" statement. An organizational vision statement or "Why" statement captures inspirationally why the organization exists at its core and what the organization wants to achieve in the future. We frequently talk about organizational vision and mission. However, as top executives, we need to start focusing on personal and professional vision statements in order to create a connection to our deeper "Why" and the reason for making changes. The step of creating a personal "Why" is often missed but it is one of the most critical for creating lasting change in both leadership and wellbeing. We know that organizations that are clear on their vision and connect deeper with their customers have engaged and motivated workforces and perform all around at a higher level. Higher performance is no different for individuals. We need to connect first to our place of possibility and vision in order to perform at our highest levels. When I shared this concept with Brad, the first thing he said was, "Great, let's think about what my vision is." When you ask most people about their vision, the first place they go is to their heads. However, when defining personal vision, this work is best done outside of the thinking brain and into the feeling body.

The heart and gut have more neurons combined than the brain, yet most people don't know how to connect to this wisdom. Connecting to the body is the access point for connecting into your deepest internal wisdom. An important concept is that you are your wisest self: The wisdom is within you. All you need are the tools and space to allow that wise self to emerge. Finding your vision is no different. Your vision is already there, you just need to connect in to access it.

The way I help people connect into their vision is through a process of guided visualization. Think about athletes in the Olympics for a moment. You see them time and time again closing their eyes and envisioning their winning run, game, or event before they compete. This is no different. Guided visualization allows you to envision what you want your winning life to look like. It connects you into possibility and into your purpose and vision. An important part of this process is closing your eyes through it, so unfortunately, I cannot take you through it while you are reading. So, before you read further, please go to www.connectedec.com/brilliant-book and download the guided visualization exercise. In this visualization, I will help you connect to your deeper vision and create a foundation for the change you are looking for in your life.

When I took Brad through this exercise, he realized his deeper vision was far greater than the goals he originally came to me with. He wanted to be a vibrant leader and father that guided people to their highest potential, including his daughters. He knew this vision was not a possibility without making some real adjustments to his current path.

Below are questions from the guided visualization exercise. Take a few moments to write down anything that came up for you during the visualization exercise.

- What's important about taking care of my whole self?

- How do I get there? What's the step that is right in front of me?

- What do I know about my vision for my life?

- What do I need to know in this moment to be successful in living my vision?

Vision statements can be written in any format. One format that has worked well for my clients is to think about it in two parts. The first part is "I am _____." The second part is "who_____." Look at how you answered the questions in the visualization for language that resonates with you. Words are powerful and have a lot of different meanings to different individuals. The word "connection" may mean one thing to you, but something very different to another person. We often think of language as very complex, but in reality, our feelings and thoughts around words go much deeper than the word itself. Try in your vision statement to find words that are powerful for you. Vision statements are often concise statements that evoke meaning within you. Here are some examples:

> *I am the energetic leader who guides people to their highest potential.*

> *I am the conduit who connects people together.*

> *I am a light who reflects kindness and grace, both personally and professionally.*

In the visualization exercise I asked your best self to give you a gift. The reason I do this is to give your brain something to anchor to on a regular basis to remember your vision statement. Some people see a word or an actual physical gift from their best self. Find a way to see your vision statement every day. If there was a physical gift in your visualization, go purchase that item and put it someplace that you will see it every day. Write down your vision statement in a place where you will see it every day. Our brains need to be trained to create new thought patterns. In order to do this, we can create physical reminders to help connect and give energy to the thoughts we want to have. A great metaphor for the brain is rain on a hillside. The first time it rains, rain will find a path down a hillside. The next time it rains, the rain naturally finds the same path down the hill. After several rainstorms, there are actual grooves in the hillside. Our brains work in the same way. Thoughts we have will repeat time and time again like the rain on the hillside finding the same grooves. If we want to find new grooves for the new thought patterns, we need to help train our brains. In order to do this, we need to give energy to new thoughts and help the brain find the new pathway we want. Creating a reminder of your vision and purpose will train the brain to have this pathway be easily accessible.

When I first left Corporate America and started my company, it was one of the biggest leaps I had ever taken in my life. I was beginning a new career that required a new way of thinking. I went through a similar visualization to that I just took you through. I saw for the first time my vision to be an executive coach and my wisest self gave me the gift of a bracelet. The next day, I ordered a silver bracelet engraved with my vision statement. My vision statement is, "I am the connected coach who reflects love and light." To this day, I wear that bracelet to remind and ground me in my own personal and professional journey. Whenever my fear becomes greater than my courage, I hold my wrist to remind me of my "Why." Our vision becomes the foundation for leadership, life, and the reason for embarking on this journey.

Another way to start connecting deeply into your wisdom and awareness is to start getting clear on your core values. Think for a moment about the principles that guide your life. Core values support your vision and become a compass for your journey. Again, think back to organizations that are clear about their core values as a company. These organizations have an easier time executing their vision and finding alignment within the organization. These companies are able to hire the talent that culturally fits well and that shares in the company's expectations with ease. Personal and leadership core values are no different. Allowing yourself to get clarity on your own core values will help you stay aligned with your vision and take actions that support your purpose. At the end of this chapter you will see a list of several words to think about. From the list, choose every core value that resonates with you. As you read through the list, simply highlight the words that feel like a core value to you professionally or personally. If you think of a value that is not on the list, write it down. You can highlight as many as you want on the first pass through the list. Once you have completed your first selections, see if you can group them into no more than five categories, putting similar words together. Choose one word within each grouping that best represents the entire group. There are no right or wrong answers. You are defining the core values that resonate for you. Once you have identified these 3–5 words, find a place to write them down where you will see them on a regular basis.

As you think about your vision and core values, recognize that the depth and information came from you and your inner wisdom. As executives, we often don't slow down long enough to listen to our best selves. We go from meeting to meeting, task to task with little time to slow down and reflect on anything. Yet our best self is there always, waiting to be accessed and listened to. What would it look like for you to create space during your day to connect to yourself differently? To slow down even for one minute or pause between meetings? This pause can take very little time but be intentional. For example, you can start your day by reading your vision statement, taking a moment to connect into your best self. Listening to our inner wisdom takes intentionality and sometimes space and curiosity. We all have the answers within us, and true change emerges from within, not from an external source.

As leaders, we have been trained to give solutions. Think about your own way of leading for a moment. When a team member comes to you with a problem, what is the first thing you want to do? Is it to provide them with the solution? For most leaders, it is. We want to solve and wonder why, when that team member hits the same roadblock, they are back in our office instead of solving it themselves. The reason is that solving problems for others doesn't create lasting change. What creates true change is bringing out a person's internal wisdom and guiding them to see it. The way to do this is through genuine listening and curiosity.

When coaches go through coaching schools, often the first thing they learn is to listen in a different dimension. Meaning we learn to listen with genuine curiosity to help our clients see their own internal wisdom. Our job as coaches is not to have the answers for our clients, but to create the space and questions to bring out what our clients already know. Our brains have a lot of thoughts happening all of the time. We often don't have great clarity on our knowledge and wisdom, because we don't have a place or time to talk through it and hear ourselves think. You can think about our brains like a hundred different people all talking at once. It is hard to know who to listen to and when. Having someone listen to you in true curiosity allows you to access your thoughts, knowledge, and wisdom in a different way.

Use Two-Dimensional Listening for Stronger Connection

Two-dimensional listening is a skill that will greatly increase your Empathetic Leadership as well. The concept of listening will be expanded as we move deeper into that second leadership level. However, the reason it is introduced here is because it is important to see the connection in how it brings out internal wisdom for our

Vital Leadership. Through two-dimensional listening, you will have more access to your own wisdom and the wisdom of others. Try this exercise: The next time you ask someone how their morning was and they respond "good," ask a follow-up question like, "What was good?" Continue down this path with this person. Put your energy on them completely and open your curiosity for them. You will be surprised by how much you learn and how quickly you learn it. You see, we spend the majority of our time engaging in one-dimensional listening. One-dimensional listening is where our energy and thoughts are all about us. We listen with the intent to respond or relate versus listening with true curiosity for the other person. Someone will share a story with us and we immediately go to share a similar story about ourselves. While this is a way to relate, it is not the deepest way to connect. Two-dimensional listening is when you put your energy and curiosity onto another person without focusing on yourself. Two-dimensional listening creates the foundation for real depth and connection with another person. It will also allow a person to connect to their individual wisdom and create deeper change as solutions emerge from within. The time we spend in two-dimensional listening is negligible. We are in such a busy culture that we rarely have anyone asking us curious questions and we certainly do not do it enough, either. To access our internal wisdom and build awareness of our self, we need to learn to listen to ourselves and others differently than we have been. Our greatest depth and potential is right there waiting to come out and be heard. You have begun accessing your best self and knowledge already through this chapter. As you spend time connecting into your vision and values daily, see if you can also begin to open your curiosity for yourself and others. Begin to explore two-dimensional listening as a tool for your leadership. The most powerful questions are often the simplest ones.

Core Values

Accomplishment
Achievement
Accountability
Accuracy
Adventure
Attitude (positive)
Beauty
Calm
Challenge
Change
Collaboration
Commitment
Communication
Community
Comfort
Compassion
Competence
Competition
Connection
Cooperation
Coordination
Creativity
Decisiveness
Delight of being, joy
Democracy
Discipline
Discovery
Diversity
Effectiveness
Efficiency
Empowerment
Excellence
Fairness
Faith
Faithfulness
Family
Flair
Flexibility
Focus
Freedom
Friendship
Fun

Global view
Good health
Gratitude
Greatness
Growth
Happiness
Hard work
Harmony
Honesty
Improvement
Independence
Individuality
Inner peace
Innovation
Integrity
Intuitiveness
Justice
Knowledge
Leadership
Learning
Love
Loyalty
Management
Maximum utilization
  (of time, resources)
Meaning
Modeling
Money
Openness
Orderliness
Passion
Peace (inner)
Perfection
Personal choice
Pleasure
Power
Practicality
Preservation
Privacy
Progress
Prosperity
Punctuality

Purpose
Recognition
Regularity
Relationships
Reliability
Resourcefulness
Respect for others
Responsibility
Results-oriented
Safety
Satisfaction
Security
Self-giving
Self-reliance
Self-thinking
Service (to others,
  society)
Simplicity
Skill
Solving problems
Speed
Spontaneity
Standardization
Status
Structure
Success (a will
  to succeed;
  achievement)
Teamwork
Techniques
Timeliness
Tolerance
Tradition
Transformation
Tranquility
Trust
Truth
Unity
Variety
Wealth
Wisdom

CHAPTER 4

Fuel Your Brilliant Leadership with the Right Food

We have begun to build the foundational awareness for Vital Leadership. Awareness of your best self, vision, and values is foundational for building your connection to self. Vitality and resiliency stem from both the awareness and the energy for self. Connecting deeply to what matters most to us is step one in our awareness. Step one in our energy starts with the foundation of food.

When I start working with a client, I complete a full personal and professional leadership assessment that highlights a leader's greatest strengths and opportunities for growth. Often this type of assessment in Corporate America is called a "360-leadership assessment" and usually only includes feedback from a leader's professional environment. My leadership assessment is a different process and entails interviewing key people in my client's professional and personal life. The reason I do a deep dive into my client's personal life as well is that being a leader doesn't mean you just show up as your best at work; it means you show up your best in life. If I am coaching someone and they are only feeling great at work and depleted at home, I have failed as a coach. The interview-based assessment process I utilize with all clients is based in positive psychology and is called "Shift +." I interview people across the organization, the board where appropriate, and the most important people in their personal lives. This allows me to understand the leader I am working with on a much more comprehensive level. At the beginning of our work together, we also complete an environmental assessment that includes an assessment of the client's office, travel environment, and home, and a full wellbeing assessment including blood work. All of these assessments help facilitate the full depth of our discovery process.

Brad and I met for a debrief of his 360-leadership assessment one afternoon in his office. He had just completed the assessment process with me, and it was time to discuss his results. As president of his company, Brad had eight direct reports and ten thousand people in his organization. I remember the first time I met Brad; I was immediately struck by his executive presence. He was well-dressed and six foot two, and I always felt like people stood up a little straighter in his presence. As I was conducting interviews about Brad, a few people shared with me that he needed to work on his executive presence. I was baffled by this feedback and of course kept asking questions to get to the bottom of the comments. What I found out was that Brad was scheduling a lot of important meetings in the 2–3 p.m. window and was actually dozing off for just a few seconds at a time, and everyone noticed when his eyes closed. When you are in a leadership position, people are always watching. Brad thought no one noticed these moments. He was wrong. In looking at Brad's blood work and also his 24-hour food log, it was clear why Brad was struggling and having the 3 p.m. slump. I was able to connect the dots for Brad around his nutrition, his energy level, and the impact on his executive presence. I could have coached Brad all day long on leadership and executive presence, but the reality was Brad was eating the wrong breakfast that was sending his blood sugar on a rollercoaster all day. He had some serious nutrient deficiencies.

Brad was equally surprised by the executive presence comments, but it all made sense once we discussed the real feedback and where it was coming from. Brad shared with me that coffee and sugar were his main source of pick-me-ups throughout the day, but his energy was completely gone by the time he got home from work. His daughters, Julie and Kayla, often wanted to play or talk the moment he walked in the door. Brad always felt sadness and guilt that he wasn't truly present with them in these moments. His girls were at the age where he knew they soon would be more interested in being with their friends. In his heart, he wanted to savor the time with them, but he never seemed to have the energy, even on the weekends. Jane, his wife, also shared with me in the 360-interview that she was worried about Brad's health and his lack of energy on the weekends. She revealed stories from their earlier years together when Brad was active and vibrant. Her hope for him was that he could reconnect to the energy he once had. In order to help Brad lead in the office and at home we started working on his knowledge of food and how food is the fuel for his energy and stamina.

Like Brad, many leaders have built their eating patterns around their daily demands and travel schedule. This can often manifest in skipping breakfast (or worse, only having coffee for breakfast), eating out for most meals, grabbing whatever food might be closest because they don't have time for lunch, or saving their entire caloric intake for dinner with a huge meal in the evening. These patterns, though immediate at satisfying hunger, actually greatly diminish overall productivity.

The brain is a blood-hungry, glucose-hungry, and oxygen-hungry organ. Because of this, the food that leaders use to fuel their body affects everything from brain function and working memory to the ability to manage complex learning tasks and reduce the risk of neurodegeneration. Many executives I work with describe the "3 p.m.

crash" that Brad was experiencing. They find themselves reaching for caffeine and sugar just so they can combat those tired feelings and finish out their day. The size of your dinner may even impact your sleep. Food has an immediate and powerful effect on energy, vitality, and overall health; that's why we start building our vital energy with nutrition as a foundation to wellbeing and leadership.

Your body and brain need an optimal mix of nutrients for optimal function. Changing your nutrition can have a profound and rapid effect on your energy levels, your sense of wellbeing, and your waistline. Fruits and vegetables contain vital nutrients that foster the production of dopamine, a neurotransmitter that plays a key role in curiosity, motivation, and engagement. Healthy food is important for energy, mental concentration, and emotional stability. The mind-body connection with food is truly a foundation of a leader's performance.

Nutrition Philosophy

My nutrition philosophy is built on two primary pillars. The first pillar is in the science of food and how nutrients work in the body, our physiology. We will explore nutrients and how to maximize nutrient density—from exploration of macronutrients (the big building blocks of our food) and micronutrients (vitamins and minerals) to how to maximize healthy food as a busy executive.

The second pillar is in the psychological and emotional connection to food. You have already become more clear on the vision of your leadership and wellbeing. This vision will be the foundation for making nutritional changes stick and creating new habits. Wellbeing is a journey and there is no need for perfection. Life happens and our health and habits can fluctuate. The important thing is that you have the tools to get back on track when you need it. You can utilize these tools no matter what your schedule looks like to create a foundation for energy, stamina, and emotional health around food.

The 80/20 rule is a guiding principle in making lasting lifestyle changes around food. This means that 80 percent of the time you focus on nutrient-dense foods that are good for your body and 20 percent of the time you focus on food that is good for your soul. By choosing 80 percent nutrient-dense foods, the 20 percent will do less damage to your physical wellbeing. I don't want you to ever deprive yourself or make foods "off limits." Depriving yourself of a food you love often leads to an unhealthy relationship with that food and the potential to binge eat. You have enough stress in your life; food does not need to add additional stress.

Nutrition is a subject with a lot of content and information. I am going to share the top three changes you can easily make in your nutrition that will impact your life and leadership the most. These three changes are the foundation of our full nutrition program and make the biggest difference in our clients' lives. Our foundations are learning your own expertise, hydration, and balancing your energy through macronutrients.

1. You Are the Expert

Nutrition has become one of the most confusing subjects because there are tons of diets, articles, and studies coming out every day, and they all seem to contradict one another. There is a reason for this: We are way behind in our understanding of food and the impact it has on the body. Here is something pretty scary to think about: Doctors, who take care of our health, have very limited training in nutrition. Most medical schools will only focus on nutrition for a day, or a week if the doctor is lucky. Then we have the people that are feeding our country, the food industry. Sadly, most food companies (not all) have prioritized profits over good nutrition. Many studies being done in nutrition are, unfortunately, funded by groups with a vested interest in the outcome—meaning the results of these studies are biased and misleading. It is becoming very difficult to discern what is credible nutrition information and what is not. The lack of nutritional knowledge, research, and focus has put us way behind in our understanding of nutrition.

First and foremost, I want you to become the expert of your body. I am here to help guide you, but a big part of this journey is listening to your internal wisdom. As you already know, the answers are within us; we just have to listen. We have become, especially as busy executives, very disconnected from how food makes our bodies feel emotionally, energetically, and physically.

When we listen closely to our inherent wisdom, we can dial into a nutrition lifestyle that is right. We are all biochemically different and foods are processed uniquely in each person. When you stick to a lifestyle that is based on whole, quality, real food and pay attention to your body, you can discover the optimal way of eating that is just right for you. "Whole, quality, real food" is food that has not been processed or refined and is free from additives or other artificial substances. We will work together to discover the foods that energize you and the ones that deplete you. Through doing the work in this chapter, you will learn to reconnect to your body and your energy through nutrition.

In order to become an expert, you have to know what you are eating. The truth is, our food has changed more in the last 50 years than it has in the last 10,000 years. Grocery stores are filled with nutritionally devoid food that tastes good but actually taxes our bodies. I am not just talking about obvious junk food such as soda, potato chips, and gummy bears, but also supposedly healthy products such as bread, pasta, prepared meals, lunch meat, and granola bars. If you look carefully at the labels, you'll see ingredients such as high-fructose corn syrup, MSG, "preservatives," and a variety of unfamiliar additives.

When I was in nutrition school, one of my projects was to deconstruct a Twinkie. My professor wanted us to understand where all of the ingredients in a Twinkie actually came from. I was shocked to learn that the food-like substances I was researching in Twinkies were all over our food system and used in products that were marketed to consumers as being healthy. Processed food is loaded with chemicals and toxins disguised with benign-sounding names. Food coloring is often made from coal. Petroleum is used as a preservative to extend shelf life and keep food "fresh" and mold-free. Olestra is a petroleum-derived oil used to extend shelf life. TBHQ is an additive that is made from butane that is often found in frozen pizzas and chicken nuggets. You'll find food-grade paraffin wax in chocolate. Cellulose is wood pulp, which adds cheap bulk to a range of products from crackers and bread, to ice cream, to shredded cheese.

Check in with your wisdom, common sense, and body. How appetizing does petroleum, coal, or wood sound? Your body isn't designed to process these things. You inherently know this, and that is the wisdom of the body. Human beings spent thousands of years eating without being told what to eat. The body knows what it needs, and if you learn to listen to it, it will guide you. Our bodies are made to digest and extract nutrition from real food. It's the stuff our ancestors would recognize and know how to prepare: fresh vegetables, fruits, nuts, grains, and meats. If you don't know an ingredient, it's likely that your digestive system and liver can't recognize or process it either.

We have one rule we use for all of our clients: If you don't know what it is, you can either look it up or not eat it. Part of this process is starting to read ingredient lists and know what food is going into your body. If you want to optimize your metabolism, you have to feed your body real food. If your brain can't comprehend it, neither can your body. Part of reconnecting to the wisdom of the body is learning to reconnect to your common sense.

One of the first challenges I gave Brad was to start reading the ingredients in his food. He started reading and looking up ingredients and quickly realized that almost all of his meals were made from "food-like" substances, not real food. Brad discovered that his favorite fast-food burger contained petroleum and wood products. Brad began to make the shift to real food and started eating a majority of meals with ingredients he knew.

I asked Brad to pay attention to how eating real foods made him feel and what impact it had on his energy. Within a few weeks, he reported feeling more energetic and "less sluggish." He also began dropping some of the weight he was carrying around his midsection. A few of Brad's senior leadership team members asked him what he was doing, because they noticed an increase in his energy and engagement. These team members assumed that it was due to the leadership coaching, but the truth was that I had only addressed Brad's nutrition at that point. Brad's leadership challenges didn't completely resolve with these nutrition changes, but little tweaks go a long way.

At the end of this chapter I have provided you with a sample page of the 7-day journal to track your food. To download the complete weekly journal, visit www.connectedec.com/brilliant-book. Use this journal to discover more about how you feel during the day, what foods support your energy, and more about what you need to feel at your best. Take time to not only write down what you eat and drink, but also record how different foods impact you throughout the day. Use this journal for the full seven days and you will be shocked at what you learn about yourself and your nutrition. We are truly the experts of our bodies and when we listen closely to our inherent wisdom, we can dial into a nutrition plan that is right for us. Remember, we are all biochemically different and foods are processed uniquely in each person. When you stick to a lifestyle that is based in whole, real food and pay attention to your body, you can find the optimal plan just for you.

2. Hydration: Creating Your Foundation to Everything

When working with leaders, one of the first things I look for are signs of chronic dehydration. Even mild dehydration can reduce memory and increase tension, anxiety, irritability, and fatigue. Studies suggest that 75 percent of Americans are chronically dehydrated. Most people simply aren't drinking enough water each day. Drinking soda or iced tea might quench your thirst, but they aren't actually a good source of hydration. This is because caffeine is a diuretic; it pulls water out of your blood and expels it through your urine. It's one step forward, two steps back. If you are drinking soda, tea, or coffee, you'll urinate out more water than you actually drink.

Water is perhaps the most underappreciated nutrient. The body is comprised of 70 percent water. There are billions of chemical processes that happen in the body every second and they all require water. Water is needed to facilitate the chemical reactions that produce energy from food, and it is essential for eliminating waste. Without adequate hydration, the heart has to work harder to push oxygen and nutrients to the brain.

Dehydration puts a strain on the entire body. When you drink less water than needed, the body rations what is available, giving precedence to the critical functions in the brain, heart, lungs, kidneys, and liver. Focus, concentration, and strategic thought may be critical for leadership, but the body doesn't see them as critical for survival.

Lots of dehydrated clients are surprised to hear that they aren't getting enough water. "But I don't feel thirsty," is something I often hear. When we are chronically dehydrated, we often are in the habit of tuning out the body's subtle pangs of thirst. Many of us mistake the sensation of thirst for hunger and we overeat rather than take a drink of water. Next time you reach for a snack, check in with your body and see if you might just be thirsty. Take a drink of water first and see if you still need that snack. The good news is that as we rehydrate our bodies, our thirst instinct will be easier to pay attention to and may even be stronger.

Hydration is one of the easiest and highest impact areas I fix with clients. Getting people to start drinking more water can dramatically impact every body function from energy, to sleep, to memory and engagement. When Brad and I discussed his hydration levels, he shared with me he didn't ever feel thirsty. He explained that his main issue was falling asleep at night and staying asleep. He was so exhausted from his sleepless nights that he had to drink caffeine throughout the day to stay engaged at work. At first glance, it appeared that Brad had sleep apnea and insomnia caused by high stress levels. Brad had a regular habit of starting the morning with two cups of coffee, drinking iced tea throughout the day, and having green tea at dinner. What Brad didn't realize is that he was drinking plenty of liquid, but the diuretic effect of the caffeine was dehydrating him. He wasn't retaining enough water. At first, I increased Brad's water intake without reducing his caffeine. This gave Brad's body a chance to hydrate without taking away his dependence on caffeine. Brad reported higher levels of energy and improvements in his sleep just from drinking more water. Proper hydration didn't solve all of Brad's sleep problems. A sleep study showed that while he didn't have sleep apnea, he did suffer from elevated anxiety at night. He needed to reduce his caffeine intake and develop mental tools to short-circuit late-night rumination. Proper hydration was foundational for getting Brad more on track with sleep.

There are a lot of factors that determine how much water someone should drink per day. Due to air quality and the high salt content in our food, a good rule of thumb is to start with your body weight and divide that number in half. That number is the number in ounces of water you should be drinking. However, here are some important things to take into consideration as well:

- Fruit and vegetable consumption: Eating a diet rich in fruit and vegetables is a great way to help your body get the hydration it needs while at the same time providing the right nutrients. The water content in fruits and vegetables is very high, so if you eat a lot of fruits and vegetables, you may not need quite as much water per day. If you do not eat a lot of fruits and vegetables, it is important to increase the amount of water you drink.

- Exercise: If you exercise, then the amount of water that is lost in your sweat will need to be replaced in addition to the daily water requirement.

- Heat: If you are in extremely hot environments—in the sun, a sauna, tanning salon, or a heated indoor room—it is important to drink additional water to replace what was depleted from sweating.

- Stress: People who have high stress levels should increase their water intake due to increased demands on the body.

- Altitude: If you live at high altitude it is important to increase your water by at least an 8-ounce glass a day.

An important note about increasing your water: If you are not at your ideal hydration level, increase your water by eight ounces every five to seven days. This helps your body adapt to the increase and keeps you from having to run to the bathroom regularly.

3. Generating Energy Balance for Your Day

As busy leaders, we often skip meals or eat on the run. We turn to sugar and caffeine, which gives us a quick energy boost and then a big crash. At meals, we tend to overload on carbohydrates, which feeds our appetite and provides our body with its preferred source of fuel (glucose), but does not give us the protein, healthy fats, fiber, and other nutrients we need to sustain our energy. There are three major nutrients that we need to eat in every meal and snack to stay healthy and well: protein, fats, and carbohydrates. These "macronutrients" (literally, big nutrients) are the major nutritional building blocks found in our food. They provide the elements needed for all body functions, including growth, metabolism, and cognition. Eating a balance of healthy macronutrients optimizes our energy, health, and capacity to think, relate, and problem-solve.

Protein is the first thing to think about for every meal. When I begin working with a new client, addressing protein often gives us a big win with very small changes. Protein is one of the main macronutrients and it impacts our entire body. It is important for maintaining strong energy levels, mood stability, and brain function. Being a leader requires strength, and protein gives us this foundation of strength.

Fat is an important nutrient that the body—and especially the brain—needs to function. Our brains are composed of 60 percent fat. Leaders often aren't getting enough healthy fat for optimal cognitive function. Flawed research turned fat into a villain in the

1970s, and the food industry began replacing healthy fat with sugar and other fillers.

Today there is a steady stream of new books and studies supporting the importance of healthy fat in the diet. Whenever we eat a source of carbohydrates, it should be accompanied by a quality source of fat because it slows down the absorption of glucose into the bloodstream and prevents sugar highs and sugar crashes.

In addition to healthy fats, our bodies need carbohydrates to function properly. Carbohydrates provide a fast-burning fuel that supports cognitive function, mood, and sleep. Fruits and vegetables are the best sources. They are high in fiber, which helps slows down the release of glucose. They also contain vital nutrients that foster the production of dopamine, a neurotransmitter that plays a crucial role in the experience of curiosity, motivation, and engagement. Fruits and vegetables are essential for energy, mental concentration, and emotional stability. This is because fruits and vegetables are packed with micronutrients (literally, "small nutrients"). Whereas macronutrients are the big vehicles for nutrition that we need to eat lots of every day, micronutrients are the vitamins and minerals that we only need in small amounts, but are essential to our health.

The most important meal of the day to energy-balance is breakfast. It fills up your empty tank and creates a strong foundation for stable metabolism, mood, and energy for the day. If you want your body and mind to function optimally, breakfast is a meal that should never be skipped. Try eating a breakfast that mixes carbohydrates with protein and healthy fats (e.g., eggs with avocado, quinoa, and grape tomatoes) and pay attention to how you feel. How does your stomach feel? How is your energy level right after you eat? How is your energy level three hours later?

When we first started changing Brad's daily nutrition, he was convinced his body just didn't need breakfast, because he was never hungry in the morning. He would often skip breakfast, barely eat lunch, and then eat a large dinner. Brad often worked late checking emails in the evening and found himself snacking on sweets to keep him going. Unfortunately, this is the exact opposite routine our bodies need. When we sleep, our bodies are recovering from the day, our immune systems are most active, our metabolisms are slower, and our brains are synthesizing the events of the day. Brad was overloading his system at night and making his body do extra work to process his heavy meals. He never woke up hungry, because he was still metabolizing his meal from the evening before. Brad started with a small breakfast to get his body used to eating in the morning. He gradually increased his breakfast size and decreased his dinner portion over time. Through these adjustments, he found he had more patience, energy, and focus throughout his day. Maintaining consistent blood sugar levels by eating a good breakfast made him hungry for lunch and eliminated almost all of the energy dips he used to feel throughout the day. When the end of the day came, for the first time in a long time, Brad felt like he even had the energy to talk to Julie and Kayla about their days with engagement and energy. His wife, Jane, noticed an immediate difference in his energy and started to see a familiar spark reignite in Brad.

At the end of this chapter I have provided you a quick reference guide for quality macronutrients. Use this guide to help you think about how to get protein, fat, and carbohydrates in every meal and snack to balance your energy, increase your stamina, and expand your Vital Leadership. I recommend taking this guide with you to the grocery store to serve as an easy reference while shopping for quality food.

Oftentimes lunch and snacks are a challenge during the workday. Schedules get packed and meetings are squeezed in during the lunch hour. Here are a few ideas for healthy packed lunches and easy snacks.

Creating Healthy Quick Lunches

1. Lettuce Wrap Sandwich

- 1/4 lb. thinly sliced turkey breast from the deli (When choosing a sliced turkey breast, be sure that it is all natural, gluten free, and does not contain any additives.)
- 1 medium/large tomato
- 1⁄4 of an avocado, sliced
- 1 head of bibb lettuce (or other large leaf lettuce)

Instructions

1. Remove lettuce leaves and rinse under cold water. Pat dry with a paper towel.

2. Wash tomato, and thinly slice. Layer turkey breast, avocado, and tomato on lettuce. Season with organic mustard or salt and pepper.

2. Chickpea Veggie Salad in a Jar

- 1 oz goat cheese (optional)
- 1⁄2 cup cooked, cold quinoa
- 1 bell pepper, chopped
- 1/2 cucumber, chopped
- 1⁄4 cup chopped carrots
- 2 oz grape or cherry tomatoes
- 5 oz chickpeas, rinsed and dried (look for organic canned)

Dressing:

- 3 tsp olive oil
- 1 tsp balsamic vinegar

- Splash of lemon juice
- Sprinkle of black pepper, salt and garlic

Instructions

1. Mason jars are a great way to take salads to work.

2. Whisk dressing in a small bowl, then transfer to the bottom of the jar.

3. Layer on top of the dressing: chickpeas, tomatoes, cucumber, carrots, bell pepper, quinoa, goat cheese.

4. Secure lid on tightly until ready to eat. Shake the jar just before eating.

3. Lemon Tahini Tuna Salad

- 3 to 4 cups chopped mixed veggies or salad greens
- 1 tbsp (15 mL) tahini
- Juice of 1 lemon
- 1/4 tsp garlic powder
- 1 can (5 oz/142 g) wild-caught tuna packed in water
- Sea salt and black pepper, to taste

Instructions

1. Place the veggies on a plate. In a medium bowl, mix the tahini, lemon juice, and garlic powder. Whisk until well combined. The dressing will be on the thick side. Add some water if needed.

2. Add the tuna to the dressing and mix gently until it's well coated. Add sea salt and pepper to taste. Spoon the tuna on top of the veggies.

Eating Easy Healthy Snacks

- Organic hardboiled eggs
- Nuts and seeds
- Kale chips
- Fruit—any kind of fresh fruit
- Vegetables—any kind of fresh vegetable
- Brown rice cakes lightly salted
- Yogurt—organic plain is preferable
- Build your own trail mix—assortment of nuts, seeds, dried fruit, yogurt chips
- Hummus and vegetables
- Chips and guacamole and/or salsa
- Cheese and crackers (whole grain)
- String cheese (organic)
- Nut butter or peanut butter and banana and/or crackers and/or celery
- Healthy bars—Perfect Bar and RXBAR are examples
- Beef/turkey jerky (organic)
- Seaweed
- Chia seed pudding

Nutrition and leadership are rarely paired together in education, conversation, or development; however, they need to be. I hope you now see the deep connection between fuel, energy, stamina, and leadership. To be our best in leadership and life we have to pay attention to our sources of energy. When we eat good food, we give our body and brain the optimal way to perform. Once we have this foundational energy, we can turn our attention to the entire body and how to leverage the wisdom it provides.

Nutrition Quick Reference

	Good Sources	Look For
Protein	**Healthy Animals** Humanely raised beef, chicken, lamb, pork, bison **Healthy Animal Products** Milk, cheese, yogurt, eggs	**Organic Label** **Beef/Dairy** Grass-fed and grass-finished **Chicken/Eggs** Pasture-raised
	Seafood	**Wild-Caught**
	Raw Nuts	**Presoaked and Sprouted** if available
	Grains and Legumes Gluten-free and properly prepared	**Gluten-Free**
Fats	**Unsaturated Fats** (liquid at room temperature) Olive, walnut, sesame, flaxseed, sunflower, peanut	**Raw Oils** Cold-pressed, dark bottles Buy only small quantities
	Saturated Fats (solid at room temperature) Grass-fed butter, ghee, coconut oil	**Healthy Animals** Organic, grass-fed, humanely raised **Coconut Oil** Extra-virgin, cold-pressed
	Avocados	**Organic** and grown as close to home as possible
	Raw Nuts and Seeds	**Presoaked and sprouted**
Carbs	**Vegetables and Fruits** Your healthiest source of carbs	**Fresh, organic and in-season**
	Gluten-free Grains Quinoa, amaranth, buckwheat, rice (brown, white, wild), millet, sorghum, teff Oats, only if labeled gluten-free	**Gluten-free label** Avoid cross-contamination with wheat for grains such as oats **Sprouted and soaked grains** Provide extra nutrients Try **brown rice pasta** as a substitution for white flour
	Legumes	When buying canned, look for **BPA-free** and **additive-free**

FOOD JOURNAL

DAY 1

Please try to keep this journal with you at all times. It is easier to record as you go rather than try to recall everything at the end of the day. At the end of 7 days, review for trends and identify one simple change you can make.

PORTION GUIDE

Fist = 1 cup
Flat palm = 3 ounces
Handful = 1 ounce

Two fingers = 1/2 cup
Thumb = 1 tablespoon
Fingertip = 1 teaspoon

	TIME	FOOD (what & how much)	DRINK (what & ounces)	EMOTIONS/ THOUGHTS	ENERGY (low) 1 2 3 4 5 (high)	
					BEFORE	AFTER
BREAKFAST						
LUNCH						
DINNER						
SNACKS						

SUPPLEMENTS

BOWEL MOVEMENTS (time of day, size & consistency)

EXERCISE (type & minutes)

OVERALL MOOD

SLEEP (hours last night)

DAILY NUTRITION (poor) 1 2 3 4 5 (good) ① ② ③ ④ ⑤

DAILY STRESS LEVEL (low) 1 2 3 4 5 (high) ① ② ③ ④ ⑤

To download the complete weekly journal, visit www.connectedec.com/brilliant-book.

PART III

Expanding into Empathetic Leadership

CHAPTER 5

Lead with Your Body to Increase Your Executive Presence

Now that you have the foundational energy you need from good fuel, it is time to talk about leveraging the full wisdom of the body to expand your leadership capacity and presence, maximizing your Vital Leadership, and expanding your capacity in Empathetic Leadership. The full body has an incredible role in leadership that is rarely tapped into. You can cultivate presence, confidence, and power through your posture and movement. Let's start with a quick exercise to drive this point home.

Take a moment and stand up. Yes, even with this book in your hand, stand up. Get into a grounded position, meaning move your feet to be hip width apart. Now, before you put this book down for this next move, read these instructions. Raise your hands into the sky and move them into a position like you just crossed a finish line at a race and are celebrating. Once you are in this position, try to think about your problems. OK, put the book down and try this exercise for a moment.

If you did this exercise with me, you probably experienced a dis- connect when you tried to think about your problems. Here is why. Our bodies and how we hold them impact our thinking. You just put your body in a position of gratitude, championship, and expansion. This change in your body position actually impacted your hormones by increasing adrenaline and testosterone (both men and women have testosterone), while at the same time the position changed the neurotransmitters that were being fired in your brain. All of the physiological changes made it hard for your brain to think about your problems. The brain would have an easier time thinking about problems if I asked you to lay down instead and put you into a fetal position, curled up in a ball.

We have learned over the past fifteen years through advances in social science, hormone monitoring, and brain mapping that our bodies have as much influence on how we think and perform as our minds. Our bodies are always trying to communicate with us and give us valuable information. Think about some of the phrases we use regularly: "My gut instinct," "I have a feeling in my bones," "Trust your gut."

We may not always be able to decipher all of the messages of our bodies, but we can listen to them and recognize the impact they have on how we lead. Embodied leadership is a relatively new term and is defined by learning to lead at a deeper, more fundamental level, working through the body to access the entire body's wisdom in leadership. It is about tuning into what our bodies are saying and utilizing our body as an access point to our greatest levels of both Vital Leadership and Empathetic Leadership.

Many of us experience the world as if we are brains with a body that is less important. The body is an appendage that we don't pay much attention to, which is a natural response to living in a time and place where the mind is valued over the body. However, sensing the body gives us a deeper and more cohesive understanding of what's taking place internally and externally. We can begin to see how our underlying felt experiences influence the quality of our thoughts. This allows us to make choices that support our wellbeing, which then can influence our performance.

One of my mentors, expert mind-body coach Chad Herst, explains, "If the body's subtle power is tapped, it can become a sensitive antenna for tuning in, whether into ourselves as a way to generate creative breakthroughs or outward to motivate and influence. The body has the potential to be a master teacher. If we listen, not only can we learn to be healthier, more vital, and more balanced, but also wiser, more compassionate, and more relatable."

An embodied approach to leadership allows you to tap into the wisdom of the body to access your greatest intuition and leadership even in the face of adversity. The expert is not outside of ourselves, it is within. When we learn to listen to and utilize the body, we grow both our capacity for self-awareness and awareness of others.

Realign Your Posture to Change Your Thinking

As Brad's energy and stamina started to increase from his nutrition, we began focusing on other aspects of his presence that needed attention. One of Brad's main concerns was his relationship with Jeff, the chairman of his company's board. Jeff seemed to always become very confrontational with Brad at their quarterly meetings. Jeff continually had more questions for Brad than anyone else and seemed to know exactly how to trigger Brad into a reaction. Brad shared with me that when talking to Jeff his thoughts never seemed clear, and every time Jeff asked deep questions on the financials, Brad's usual excellence in financial data seemed to go out the window. I asked Brad to start paying attention to his body before and during the board meetings and notice how he was feeling and how he was holding his body throughout the meeting. At our next meeting, Brad shared with me that before the meeting he noticed a lot of anxiety in his gut and during the meeting he had a tendency to slump in his chair. He realized that his slumping was an attempt to avoid confrontation with Jeff. However, it never worked. What Brad didn't realize at the time was that his body was communicating important information and his body posture during the meeting was solidifying his lack of clarity and confidence.

Learning to listen to the body gives us the greatest access to our presence as a leader. We used to think of executive presence as only others' perception of our leadership capabilities. Now we understand that how we hold our bodies impacts more than just other people's perception of us. Our bodies actually impact our confidence levels, how well we communicate, and how clearly we think. Amy Cuddy, social psychologist, professor, and researcher at Harvard Business School, has done some incredible research showing the connections between body posture and presence. In her book *Presence*, Cuddy cites many studies showing us that our body language not only shapes the way other people see us, but also shapes how we see ourselves. Holding our bodies in expanded, open positions that Cuddy refers to as "power poses," increases our testosterone, lowers our cortisol levels, and increases our adrenaline. This hormonal effect impacts how we feel and how we think, especially in higher stress situations. By standing in expanded postures, we actually feel stronger and more powerful in our bodies and in our thoughts.

Cuddy's research proves the importance of aligned body posture in our confidence and executive presence. How we sit and stand both makes a statement about ourselves to others and gives us a particular experience of ourselves. When a person sits or stands in a correct body alignment with our head aligned over our shoulders (not jutting forward), our hips in alignment and the top of our head reaching to the sky, our bodies give us a sense of confidence and ease. Cuddy's research at Harvard University showed evidence that participants who had their backs taped to be in a correct postural alignment performed better in mock interviews than those who had not.

Think for a moment how we normally hold our bodies during the day. Grab your phone and look at it. What is your body position? Are your shoulders rounded, your head slumped forward, your back rounded and slouched? Are you more in the fetal position? How often do you look at your phone every day? We are in the digital age, where we spend a significant amount of time in front of computers and looking at our phones. This puts our bodies continually out of alignment and closes us off. This alignment puts us out of touch with our ability to connect and to be connectable.

"Many of us believe that the body's center of gravity lies somewhere behind the eyes, when our actual center of gravity is about two to three inches below the navel," explains mind-body expert Herst. "This understanding allows yogis and martial artists to cultivate balanced and centered postures. The resulting stability enables them to defend themselves, throw their opponents, or twist into acrobatic poses. It also translates into mental, emotional, and interpersonal strength."

Embodied leadership is the practice of utilizing the body to impact how a leader thinks and acts in the world. Ben King, embodied leadership coach and master trainer, shares that an aligned posture can balance and center you, making creativity, decision making, and confidence all more accessible. King explains that a centered posture also impacts others' perception of your executive presence. Research shows that posture affects hormones in both humans and animals. In one study, subjects assuming either a contracted or expansive pose for just one minute reported feeling either more stressed or more powerful, and their neuroendocrine systems registered hormonal spikes as well.

Brad and I discussed ways to improve his relationship with Jeff. The first thing I wanted Brad to work on was how he utilized his body during those board meetings. Before the meeting I asked Brad to utilize Cuddy's research by adopting the power pose. Brad laughed at me at first and asked if I really wanted him to stand in the board room in a Superman stance as everyone walked in. I told him to find somewhere private to get his body and mind in the right place before he walked into the meeting. We agreed that he could draw the blinds of his office and power pose in there. Next I asked him to pay attention during the meeting and try to keep his body in a more aligned, expansive posture even while sitting down. After the board meeting, Brad called me very excited. "It worked!" Brad shared with me that he felt more centered as he walked into the room and had a positive interaction with Jeff even before they started the meeting. Then in the meeting Jeff started asking financial questions like usual, but they didn't feel as confrontational, and there were far fewer than usual. It was the most successful board meeting Brad had ever had. He was surprised that just this awareness of his body could change the dynamics of a meeting so greatly.

What Brad didn't understand before our coaching was that his slumped posture in the meeting was actually increasing his anxiety and stress. The more our bodies contract, the more cortisol pumps into our blood supply, generating feelings of anxiety and tension. We are seen as timid and we experience ourselves as holding back in some way. Our bodies are always communicating with us and with others.

What percentage of communication do you believe the words we speak actually are? Surprisingly, it is only 7 percent of our communication. Body language is 55 percent and voice tone is the other 38 percent. We are communicating with our body language constantly and we need to be more aware of what we are saying. For example, consistent eye contact shows confidence and can create deeper connections by demonstrating engagement and understanding. The body can be utilized as a tool for learning and changing the way we deal with all situations, whether they are personal or interpersonal, physical, or emotional. Through exploration of how we hold our body and understanding the power of posture, we can utilize the body to align ourselves both physically and mentally.

One of the small things you can do every day is be more conscious of how you are holding your body and your body posture. Whether you are in your car, at your desk, in a meeting, or at an event, pay attention to your head, shoulders, and back. Can you move into better alignment? A couple of easy ways to move into alignment are given below.

Create a Healthy Sitting Posture

- Keep your feet on the floor, or on a footrest if they don't reach the floor.

- Don't cross your legs. Your ankles should be in front of your knees.

- Keep a small gap between the back of your knees and the front of your seat.

- Your knees should be at or below the level of your hips.

- Adjust the backrest of your chair to support your lower and middle back or use a back support.

- Relax your shoulders and keep your forearms parallel to the ground.

- Keep your shoulders pulled backward and down, and your head reaching toward the sky.

- Avoid sitting in the same position for long periods of time.

Desk Considerations

- Your chair height should allow you to sit tall with your shoulders relaxed and pulled back and your forearms parallel to the ground or lower. You shouldn't need to reach up to your keyboard or shrug your shoulders.

- Your desk chair should support your lumbar spine. If not, consider getting a support pillow or new chair.

- Your monitor height should allow you to look straight ahead without having to adjust your neck angle to view the screen.

Align Your Standing Posture

- Bear your weight primarily on the balls of your feet.

- Keep your knees slightly bent.

- Keep your feet about shoulder-width apart.

- Let your arms hang naturally down the sides of the body.

- Stand straight and tall with your shoulders pulled backward and down, with your head reaching toward the sky.

- Tuck your stomach in.

- Keep your head level; your ear should be in line with your shoulders. Do not push your head forward, backward, or to the side. If you have to stand for a long time, shift your weight from your toes to your heels, or one foot to the other. Try to keep your hips in a neutral position, meaning not tilted forward or back.

Access the Power of the Breath to Become Responsive

One of the most powerful embodied leadership tools is actually something we have used from the moment we were born: our breath. It is a tool that can be utilized in any situation to become a more present, responsive leader. In *The Wizard of Oz*, Dorothy finds out that her ruby slippers, the shoes she has been wearing all along, are what can bring her home. Like Dorothy's slippers, the breath is the most powerful leadership tool there is, and it has been with us all along. I want to show you first the different types of breathing we utilize on a regular basis. Put one hand on your chest and one hand on your stomach. Now take a few breaths. Notice which hand raised. Was it the hand on your chest or your stomach? Now, I want you to imagine there is a balloon in your stomach that you are trying to blow up. Take a breath and see if you can get the hand on your stomach to raise. What you are doing by raising the hand on your stomach is called a diaphragmatic breath, and it is the best leadership tool there is.

Most people are in what we call an inverse breathing pattern due to the excess of stress and stimulation we face every day. Our breath actually should naturally be 70 percent in the diaphragm and 30 percent in the chest with each breath. Most people breathe in the opposite proportions of this ratio. While the diaphragm is not in the stomach, it helps to think of the diaphragmatic breath taking place in the stomach area for practicing this type of deep breathing technique. The diaphragm is a dome-shaped respiratory muscle found near the bottom of your ribcage, right below your chest. When you inhale, your diaphragm contracts (tightens) and moves downward. This creates space in your chest cavity, allowing the lungs to expand and take in more oxygen. When you exhale, your diaphragm relaxes and moves upward in the chest cavity. When we breathe with the diaphragm it keeps our nervous system calm. There are two important parts of the nervous system—the sympathetic nervous system, which prepares the body for a physical reaction to a real threat (fight, flight, or freeze) and the parasympathetic nervous system, which is responsible for rest and digestion.

A diaphragmatic breath actuates the parasympathetic nervous system within the body. Here is one of the most interesting facts about our bodies: They do not know the difference between emotional stress and physical stress. We actually are still wired like we are living back in caveman times. When we have a stressful situation at work, our bodies are still physiologically reacting like there is a tiger about to eat us. Our bodies respond by activating the sympathetic nervous system and we get ready to go into fight or flight mode. Our brains get into reactive mode and we often in these times say or do things we wish we hadn't. Our neurobiology has not caught up with the circumstances we find ourselves in today. Our sympathetic nervous system is designed to help us get excited about things and to avoid threats to our lives. Biologically speaking, our brains were not designed for as much sympathetic excitement as we give them these days. Everywhere we turn, our nervous systems are getting stimulated, whether we are downing our caffeine drinks, reacting to every ring and buzz emitted from our mobile phones, or reading the bad news of the day. This is the reason so many of us are in an inverse breathing rhythm. When we are in the sympathetic nervous system, our chest breathing is activated. If something startles you, where does your breath go? It goes into your chest to prepare you for fight or flight.

Diaphragmatic breathing moves our bodies and minds back into a state of calm. Just by taking one breath, you can elicit a relaxation response in the body. Diaphragmatic breathing also strengthens your core muscles, brings your body naturally back into alignment, and helps your posture. Consciously breathing deeply and slowly into the stomach rather than the chest is a powerful and easy way to balance the nervous system. Diaphragmatic breathing increases your capacity to find calm and, at the same time, be energetic. In a study comprised of twenty-one soldiers (an active group of eleven and a control group of ten), those who received a one-week training in conscious breathing techniques showed lower anxiety, reduced respiration rates, and fewer PTSD symptoms.

Using this type of breathing can help your body and brain handle stressful situations with ease, calm, and clarity. As we have discussed, the body is in the driver's seat a lot more than we ever realized. When we are in a state of high pressure and stress our bodies take over. If we do not intentionally let the body know it is safe through our breathing, we could become reactive and stay in a state of fight or flight. Leadership from a reactive state of mind and body is not powerful leadership.

Diaphragmatic breathing allows you to access your window of calm. Think about a young child who has lost control and is in a tantrum. What is the first thing we usually say to that child? Take a deep breath. Now you know why generations have been parenting children with the wisdom of the breath. It works! Now you can impact your leadership presence and capabilities with this tool.

To practice diaphragmatic breathing, do the exercise below. Once you have become skilled at the diaphragmatic breath, you can use it any time and change your state of mind. It usually only takes one intentional breath.

Use This Two-Minute Diaphragmatic Breathing Exercise Every Day:

1. Find a posture that is both steady and comfortable, whether sitting in a chair, cross-legged on the floor, or lying down.

2. Place one hand on your chest and the other on your belly, just below the navel.

3. As you breathe in, attempt to make the hand on the belly move while keeping the hand on the chest immobile. Doing so will activate the diaphragm. As you exhale, the belly hand will fall.

4. Once you get the hang of expanding the diaphragm, start to regulate your inhale and exhale by inhaling for a count between three and five seconds. Make sure that:

    a. Both inhalation and exhalation are equal.
    b. You manage to take a full in-breath and out-breath.
    c. You do not strain.

When Brad was in his board meeting after our embodiment coaching, the other tool he had was the knowledge of his breath. After Jeff's first financial question, he took a diaphragmatic breath to keep his body calm and focused. The work he had done to get grounded before the meeting stuck with him. Brad utilized the breath to not let Jeff move him into a reactionary space. Brad was beginning to see how his awareness of the body made him a more Vital Leader and able to handle any situation he faced.

Create Movement in Your Day to Improve Your Health, Productivity, and Clarity

If you are like most leaders, you spend much more time sitting than moving. You sit in meeting after meeting all day long. You sit on long-haul flights and in short-haul commutes. You sit in front of the computer. You sit for meals. At night, you unwind in front of the TV. This much sitting is terrible for the body and mind. And there's plenty of science to prove it.

After about thirty minutes of sitting, your metabolism slows by 90 percent. Your body drops into a kind of hibernation state, just like a bear in winter, where whatever you ate for your last meal is more likely to end up as stored fat around your waist than as fuel to boost your energy level. Prolonged sitting has been shown to have a negative effect on the heart, insulin production, and colon health. It weakens the abdominal muscles, tightens the back and hips, and softens the glutes, all of which hurts your posture. When we are sedentary for a long time, everything slows down, including blood circulation, digestion, and brain function.

Many people believe the best way to get movement into their life is the one-hour workout that many people struggle to include in their busy schedules. Working the body for a prolonged period can have positive effects to cardiovascular health, lower cortisol levels, and increase hormonal wellbeing; however, vigorous exercise can't compensate for the damage incurred by prolonged daily sitting. If you work out every morning, but sit the rest of the day, your body still goes into hibernation mode.

One of the things I hear most often from clients is there is no time in the day for a workout. We have been trained over the years to think if we can't find time to work out for an hour, then we might as well not do anything at all. This is actually the exact opposite of how we should be thinking about movement. A body in motion stays in motion and a body at rest stays at rest. If we find small opportunities to move in our day, it will help us mentally, physically, and emotionally. Small movement encourages the body to seek more movement. We need to move away from the all-or-nothing mentality and stop our pattern of sitting all day long.

When I first got promoted to VP, I took on a lot of travel and late hours. There weren't enough hours in the day for everything I had to do. Something had to give, and the first thing I gave up on was my workouts. Like many people, I believed anything less than a full hour at a gym didn't seem worth the bother. After months of not working out regularly, I felt sluggish and longed to feel strong again. A lifelong athlete, I didn't imagine that it would be hard to start back into an exercise program. But for the first time in my life, I couldn't will myself into action. It was profoundly humbling, and truth be told, I felt ashamed.

Realizing that I lacked the energy and time for the intense workouts I did while training for triathlons, I started small by increasing the amount of low-intensity movement in my day. I began standing during phone calls and took short "walking breaks" several times a day. Then I found a gentle yoga class a few mornings each week. This helped me de-stress and build back my stamina. Little by little, I found my way back into a more intense movement routine. Through finding my physical strength, I also found new emotional strength.

When I had been feeling at my lowest physically, I found myself showing up poorly in my professional life with a short fuse. When I began moving physically again, I found I was more open, positive, and confident. My team noticed that I was in a better head space as well. There is a great saying: "Move your body and your mind will follow." Through rediscovering movement, I found a connection to my authentic leadership style again.

Movement keeps us healthy, happy, and energized. However, we are sitting more now in the workplace than we ever have. I want you to think about how you can bring movement back into the culture of your workplace. It can be simple things like inviting people to stand in a meeting if they want to and you taking the lead to be the example. Just moving your body can create new openings in the conversation and perspectives. When you have one-on-one meetings, be willing to change them to a walking meeting, even if that means walking in the building. Consider getting a standing desk and/or make sure your workspace is set up to help your posture. Take the stairs more often. Try stretching on a phone call either in your seat or standing up. Set a timer for every 20–30 minutes that makes you get up and move. This will make sure you don't stay in the same position too long. You can also use this timer to remind you to drink water. We can no longer say that we can't move our bodies because we don't have enough time. This is only further disconnecting us from the wisdom our bodies have to offer, and also hurting our health.

Take Time to Stretch at Your Desk

Neck: Slowly flex your head forward and backward and side to side, and look right and left. This can be done almost any time to lessen tension and strain. Never roll your head around your neck. This could cause damage to the joints of the neck.

Shoulders: Roll your shoulders forward around ten times, then backward ten times. This helps release the tension in your shoulders.

Arms: Sit upright, then lift the right arm overhead, keeping your elbow straight. Bend slowly to the left side, then lift the left arm and stretch to the right side.

Wrists: Roll the wrists ten times clockwise, then ten times counterclockwise. If you spend a lot of time typing, this will help minimize the potential for getting carpal tunnel syndrome.

Calves: While sitting, lift up your legs on the balls of your feet and set them down. Repeat until your legs are comfortably tired. Repeat ten minutes later; continue for about an hour. This will help prevent blood clots from developing in your legs.

Hamstrings: Sit tall in your chair, straighten out your left leg, and flex your ankle so your toes are pointing up. Tip your pelvis forward to apply a greater stretch to the back of your leg. Repeat five times; then do the same on your other leg.

Ankles: As with your wrists, roll the ankles in a clockwise motion three times, then counterclockwise. This helps improve blood circulation, and prevents that tingling feeling you can get when blood circulation is cut off, also known as "pins and needles."

Find Exercise Again and Lower Your Stress

When Brad and I first started talking about movement as an access point to his leadership, he looked at me a little sideways. He was unclear on how movement during the day would actually kick-start his performance and desire to move more. He had seen the impacts of his body language, posture, and breath, so he agreed to start taking the stairs once a day and finding one meeting to either do walking or standing once a week. Little by little Brad started walking and standing more. It wasn't a huge change all at once. Brad gradually started incorporating more opportunities to move his body and started to feel the effects not only in his physical body, but also the clarity of his thoughts. He reported that his biggest surprise was with a one-on-one meeting he had with a direct report with whom he was really struggling with at the time. He had several meetings with Donna discussing her leadership opportunities, but never felt like the conversations landed well or that she made improvements in her leadership. He recommended they shift their one-on-one meetings to walking meetings instead. Donna happily agreed. Brad reported that their conversations seemed much deeper and both Donna and Brad experienced breakthroughs in their relationship together. Donna also was able to gain a better perspective on her leadership opportunities and opened up to Brad and asked him for help. Walking outdoors increases movement, and being in nature and other changes of scenery creates new neuropathways which can yield new ideas and new solutions to problems.

After a few months of Brad incorporating movement into his workday he felt ready to prioritize a regular exercise routine in the morning. My first question to him was, "What do you enjoy doing?" He shared that he always loved riding a bike. Unfortunately, it was the middle of winter and riding outside was not an easy option. We brainstormed on ideas and landed on purchasing the Peloton bike. The Peloton is a stationary spin bike and many gyms offer group classes using them. At first Brad committed to just ten minutes three times a week on the bike. He gradually increased his time and days and attended a regular weekend spin class at his gym. After only about nine months with his new bike, he signed up to ride the MS 150, which is a 150-mile bike ride supporting people with multiple sclerosis. There is no way Brad could have committed to this race when we first started talking about movement. It was the small steps he took to get his body in motion that led him to accomplish this goal.

Once your body has found more motion throughout the day, you may decide it is time to prioritize a regular, more vigorous exercise routine. We are built to get joy and pleasure from movement and exercise. Think of how it felt as a kid to ride a bike, swim at the beach, play a game of tag, jump on a trampoline, or dance with friends. As adults, high-intensity movement can help us burn off stress, clear our minds, and increase our levels of serotonin, the "feel good" neurotransmitter.

When we do not feel good about ourselves, many of us turn to a drill sergeant. We either employ our inner sergeant or we hire someone to beat us into submission. Either way, this approach fails miserably. Self-loathing is stressful on the body and it prompts our adrenals to pump out the stress hormone cortisol. A steady drip of cortisol leads to depression, and depression isn't very motivating. Drill sergeants, whether internal or external, aren't sustainable. If you push yourself too hard, you eventually burn out. We're under enough pressure at work; movement should be a pleasure, not a chore.

What do you think is the very best exercise you can do? I mean the one that time and time again has been proven to be most effective? The answer is actually very simple; it is the one you love and will continue to do. Part of the journey is to discover what that is for you. I invite you to be playful in the process of trying new things and discovering what exercise you truly enjoy.

For many people, movement is easier in the company of others, whether with a trainer or in a group class. Moving with others can be a powerfully bonding experience. An Oregon State University study showed that the closer a teacher's movement coordinated with his or her students, the more the students felt positive rapport.

Moving together makes us feel connected to one another. In another study, participants not only felt more connected but also better about themselves following a period of synchronized movement, compared to those who performed unsynchronized movement. It appears that moving in time with others may result in feeling better about ourselves.

There is no one-size-fits-all exercise program for great leadership. Different things work for different people. What matters is that you do something you can enjoy over the long term.

Sleep Well, Wake Well

The vast majority of the executives with whom I work come to me suffering from chronic exhaustion. Ninety-eight percent of people need seven to eight hours of sleep every night to be healthy. That means that only 2 percent of the population needs less than seven to eight hours. I can tell you 75 percent of executives believe they are in the 2 percent.

Healthy food choices and regular physical movement play an important role in helping to increase energy levels, but without adequate rest every day, you just aren't going to feel good. It's rare for me to see a leader who isn't sleep-deprived. Some have difficulty falling asleep. Others struggle to stay asleep. Still others go down for the count, but the quality of their sleep is so poor that they awake in the morning feeling exhausted.

According to Matthew Walker, the director of the Center for Human Sleep Science at the University of California, Berkeley, "Every disease that is killing us in developed nations has causal and significant links to a lack of sleep." He points out that lack of sleep—defined as six hours or fewer—can have serious consequences.

Sleep deficiency is associated with problems in concentration and memory, and a weakening of the immune system. It may even shorten life span. Based on research, losing two hours of sleep from the recommended seven to eight hours has the same impact on concentration and reaction time as drinking two to three beers.

On the whole, we're living in times where sleep is harder to get. We're made to sleep when it's dark and quiet and wake when it's light. Artificial light, noise, and mental stimulation at night interrupt our natural sleep rhythms. We're sleepy when we should be alert and alert when we should be resting. As a result, many of us are turning to sleep aids. Some reports estimate a tripling in sleep aid prescriptions for young adults since the late '90s. Unfortunately, sleeping pills and alcohol do not restore us the way natural sleep does. While alcohol can knock us out, it also wakes us up throughout the night and seems to block REM sleep, the sleep that helps us stay sane.

The two main issues I see in executives are trouble falling asleep and then frequent wakeups in the night. These two issues are usually caused by different problems. Problems falling asleep are usually attributed to sleep routines, while trouble staying asleep is typically caused by poor nutrition, stress, and a challenging sleep environment.

Brad, unfortunately, struggled with both falling asleep and staying asleep. Brad shared with me that he was consistently waking up at least four or five times per night for short periods. He would awaken and then start spinning in his head about different issues affecting him at work. I did a home tour for Brad to see if there were any glaring issues with his sleep environment. I found one the moment I walked into his bedroom. Brad lived in a busy city with lots of lights and sounds, but his bedroom windows didn't have blinds. He was also taking NyQuil each night to fall asleep. Without it, his brain would race even before bed.

Once Brad realized that his lack of blinds was an issue, he immediately ordered some. We also changed some of his sleep routines before bed to help his nervous system relax. He began turning off all screens an hour before bed, taking a hot bath, and reading a book. With his new routine in place we were able to move him to a natural sleep aid as a first step. I also had Brad keep a journal by his bed to help him write down some of the racing thoughts he was having. This gave his mind the ability to release the thought instead of spinning on it.

After about two months, Brad started to be able to fall asleep on his own without sleep aids and to get a consistent six hours. Once Brad had consistency in his nutrition and his blood sugar was stabilized, he was able to get seven to eight hours a night.

Good sleep hygiene practices are essential for leaders. What we eat and drink in the later part of the day can interfere with our ability to sleep. Sleep experts recommend avoiding caffeine after 2 p.m., limiting alcohol consumption, and eating a light, easy-to-digest dinner. Your sleep environment should be dark, quiet, and cool. Good sleepers have a bedtime routine that downshifts them into a restful state.

If you're not sleeping well, it's important to pinpoint what's going on. Blood work and sleep studies can identify medical issues (such as sleep apnea) or nutritional deficiencies that interfere with restful sleep. If you don't have a good way to deal with underlying anxiety, sleep is going to be tough. The most important thing is that you not accept a lifetime of sleep deprivation. Below are a few recommendations to get your sleep back on track.

Environment

- Limit light pollution and noise in your bedroom.
- Cooler temperatures help create better sleep.

Routine

- Maintain a consistent bedtime and wakeup time. Ten p.m. to 6 a.m. is optimal.
- Create a bedtime ritual that helps you wind down from the day (e.g., baths, herbal tea, candles, reading, journaling, and meditation).
- No screens at least 30 minutes prior to bed.
- Keep paper and pen next to your bed for ideas and to-dos that wake you up. Writing them down will help you relax and fall back to sleep.

Nutrition and Hydration

- Stay hydrated throughout the day, but limit water intake close to bedtime.
- A diet rich in nutrients will improve the release of serotonin in the gut for better sleep.
- If you are waking up 4 1/2 to 6 hours into your sleep, eat a small quantity of protein (approximately three grams) thirty minutes prior to bed to balance blood sugar throughout the night.

Exercise and Breath

- Regular exercise will improve your ability to fall asleep and stay asleep.

- Use diaphragmatic breathing to calm the nervous system and get your body ready for sleep. It will also help you to fall back to sleep during wakeups. You can also count backwards to relax the mind while focusing on your breathing.

As leaders, we need to find the things that give us energy and recharge. If sleep didn't make the list on your energy replenishment worksheet, go back and add it now. So much of our day has us sending energy out. Recharging is about bringing energy in. Sleep is an essential part of healing the body, nourishing the mind, and replenishing our energy. Our energy is truly the foundation of our wellbeing and leadership. When the foundation is solid, we have the ability to come back to it over and over again, even in times of high change and pressure. Our strong physical bodies create the resiliency for our minds.

CHAPTER 6

Practice a Postive Mindset to Build Resiliency

Brad's journey into feeling vital was working. His most recent physical came back showing incredible improvements in his cholesterol, blood sugar, hydration, and inflammatory markers. Brad's wellbeing and energy were continually improving. It was time to expand further into Empathetic Leadership and turn our attention to the quality of thoughts in his mind, his ability to manage the fast pace of change and stress he was facing on a daily basis, and his desire to connect more with his team.

Brad was a leader that had incredible care for everyone around him. As I got to know Brad's authentic style, it was clear to me what a kind man I was working with. Through my leadership interviews for Brad, I learned that the man I was seeing was not seen by many people Brad interacted with. People reported to me that they felt intimidated by Brad, that he rarely listened, and that they didn't feel or see his care for people. His leadership team felt he was very harsh in his language and would explode unexpectedly during meetings, especially in times of high pressure and change in the organization. In Brad's business, it seemed there was always high pressure and change. Jane, his wife, also shared with me that Brad seemed to get stuck in patterns of negative thinking that he couldn't snap out of, especially right after work. The more Jane encouraged him to snap out of it, the more frustrated he got. His level of stress was continually growing from his loops and patterns of negative thinking. It was clear that we needed to help Brad understand his own thoughts and emotional landscape, while at the same time help him connect with those around him at a deeper level. In leadership development, we often talk about resiliency as a key to success, stress reduction, and performance. In order to help Brad grow in this critical dimension of leadership, I needed to help him understand how to be a master of his own mind.

Understanding Resiliency

The reason we talk so much about resiliency in business and in leadership is that having resiliency has been cited as one of the top determiners of high performance. Having the capacity to be resilient leads to more flexibility, better problem solving, more optimism, higher levels of creativity, and, of course, better stress management. The great news is that if we are not born with high levels of emotional resiliency, we can utilize tools to grow our capacity.

Let's first talk about what resiliency actually is. Resiliency is defined as the capacity to recover quickly from difficulties, which is sometimes referred to as toughness. When we think of resilience in a person, we often define it as a person's capacity to respond to pressure and the demands of daily life. The reason you are hearing this word so often in the workplace these days is that resiliency at work is now recognized as one of the top characteristics for an engaged, thriving workforce. The best leaders aren't infallible; they are resilient. They understand that change and pressure are part of life and they draw upon their inner wisdom and their foundation to face it. Strong Vital Leadership creates the needed foundation to support our greatest resiliency.

The strains and pace of change we face in the modern workplace makes resiliency an essential characteristic for handling stress. The question is: How do we grow our resiliency? Our bodies have a natural physical resiliency to them. Think about what happens when you break a bone. Your body naturally works to heal it. Or how about when you get sick? Your body's immune system takes over to help you feel better. We are all born with physical resiliency. How about emotional resiliency? Are some of us born with higher capacities? The answer is yes. Some people are born with higher capacities for emotional resiliency while others have to be intentional to grow in this important characteristic.

Parenting my two children, Jack and Ella, has taught me more about resiliency and growing our capacity for it than anything else in life. Learning to parent these two very different humans has taught me just as much, if not more, than my leadership career and work. Jack is my 10-year-old boy, who I often say is like a 45-year-old man in a 10-year-old's body. Jack's interests, even at four years old, included business, the weather, and car washes. At 10 years old, his interests haven't changed. Jack is always looking into the future and thinking about new, innovative ideas. Ella is my 8-year-old daughter. Ella has a presence and joy for life that is absolutely incredible to watch. She dances in the moment, lets things roll off her back, and has a natural grace when approaching life.

Ella came into this world with a natural ability to be present in the moment and handle the ups and downs of life. I remember her coming home from school one day and sharing with me that she had done a cartwheel in front of one of her friends. Ella's cartwheel was a work in progress at the time. I asked what her friend had said after Ella's cartwheel. Ella happily said, "My friend said it was terrible." My heart sank for Ella. I quickly asked Ella, "How did that make you feel?" With a huge smile she said, "I didn't care what she thought. I love doing cartwheels." That story exemplifies the natural orientation of my daughter. As a parent, I don't have to think about building her resiliency on a regular basis. Resiliency comes naturally and easily to Ella. Jack, my son, is in a different category. As I mentioned, Jack is always thinking about the future. At ten years old he has already had four businesses, is invested in the stock market, and would watch the news every day if I let him. His gift is in future-oriented, innovative thinking, but, unfortunately, that thinking also creates anxiety. We started to see anxiety in Jack at a fairly young age. We decided at six to take him to play therapy to help him learn how to work with his own mind. The first time we went to play therapy, I sat on a couch waiting for Jack as he worked with the therapist behind closed doors. After the session finished, Jack walked out. I was nervous to hear what Jack thought of the session. I couldn't read the expression on his face to know whether he liked the session or not. As we walked down the stairs away from the office, he looked at me and asked, "Did you pay for that Mom?" Confused by the question coming from my six-year-old, I explained that I did. He then asked, "How much did you pay for that Mom?" I told Jack that I paid $150 for the session. His response: "Well next time she better give me some tools then, because all we did for the last hour was play." I burst out laughing. Though a great strategy for some, play therapy was not the right fit for Jack. What Jack was asking for was actually Cognitive Behavioral Therapy (CBT), which is what we eventually found for him. In CBT Jack learned the tools to work with his anxiety through the mind and body.

This topic became important to me on so many levels. As a leadership coach, I am often asked how to help build resiliency in leaders and teams, and my answer is that to build resiliency we need two things: a strong foundation and a model on how to actually build it. Jack and Ella were the greatest teachers in helping me build a resiliency model that made sense at any age.

One of the most influential books I've read on this topic was *Work without Stress: Building a Resilient Mindset for Lasting Success* by Derek Roger and Nick Petrie. In their book, Roger and Petrie talk about above the line and below the line mindsets. Their discussion of this line and the understanding of our mind's propensity to ruminate was influential to my model on resiliency. Evan Roth, another executive coach who specializes in the C-suite and a dear friend, was also a collaborator on the model I am about to share with you.

Here is the foundation: The only thing that never changes is that change is inevitable. Being a person in this world means that you are going to face pressure and change. It doesn't matter if you are a teacher, flight attendant, or CEO, change and pressure are an unavoidable part of life. How you respond to that change and pressure is your choice. Through this model, you will see how to become aware of where your thoughts tend to go and how to choose where you put your energy. Following is the resiliency model I use with both my son and my clients.

	PAST	Being Present	FUTURE
Positive	Reflection Reminiscing		Planning Strategy Innovation
	PRESSURE/CHANGE/LIFE		
Negative	Regret Guilt	Stress / Rumination	Worry Anxiety Negative Forecast

The center bar represents an event, a situation, general pressure and/ or the various changes we experience in life. When we are below the line in our thinking in these areas, our minds run away with our thoughts. We spin without awareness into negative thinking loops. This is called rumination. When we spend time in rumination, either unaware or aware of our thought patterns, it leads to stress, meaning our bodies physically start eliciting a stress response. As we discussed, emotional stress and physical stress impact the body and mind in similar ways. When we are in rumination cycles, the mind and body are stressed. When we move our thinking above the line into the present moment with positive thought patterns, we can eliminate or reduce that stress.

Let's break down this model even further. We all have a tendency to be either past-oriented or future-oriented in our thought patterns. If we look at what past thinking looks like below the line (bottom left quadrant), we can see negative patterns of replaying past situations over and over in our mind. This is usually a negative thought pattern of guilt or regret. Sitting in continual feelings of guilt or regret about something you said or did doesn't lead to anything good in life or wellbeing. Yet we sit for hours in these thought patterns, sometimes unaware of our thinking and the impact our thoughts are having on our mental wellbeing. We let our thoughts take over without the realization that we are actually the masters of our own mind, and we have a choice.

When we move our past-oriented thinking to above the line (top left quadrant), we see opportunities for reflection, lessons learned, and reminiscing. I am not saying that we never make mistakes or when we do, we don't need to think about them. What I am saying is we need to reflect, learn, grow, and move forward without torturing our minds with the past. Resiliency is about facing a challenge and being able to grow and move forward from it.

Now let's look at the right side, future-oriented energy and thinking. When we are below the line in this area we are worried about the "what ifs." We think about the future with a negative forecast, which creates worry and anxiety. People with a lot of future-oriented energy also tend to be people who are innovative and can see around the corners in life. When we move patterns of anxious thinking above the line, we can focus on planning, innovation, and strategy. My son, Jack, has a ton of future-oriented energy and thinking. It is truly his gift. He is one of the most innovative children I have ever known. He thinks about his future more at ten years old than I did in my twenties. However, all of this wonderful thinking and energy can easily slip him into anxiety. When Jack's thoughts go below the line, his worry about the future takes over. I utilize this model a lot with him. When I notice Jack slipping below the line, I gently acknowledge that his thoughts and energy seem to be below the line. I always ask him, "What would it look like to use that energy above the line?" A great example of this is his struggle with homework. When Jack gets a lot of homework on his plate, he feels stressed. He worries about how he is going to get it all done in one week. If he continues with these worried thought patterns, it will send him into full anxiety. My question to him in these moments is, "What would be helpful to get you above the line?" This usually leads us into planning the week out into small chunks to get his homework done. No matter what our age is, worry and negative thinking about the future doesn't help us lead or live well.

Resiliency of our minds is built through staying above the line as much as possible. The first step in this process is to become aware of when our thinking is below the line. Sometimes we are in what the authors of *Work Without Stress* call "wakeful sleep." Meaning we are awake, but completely unaware of our thoughts and sometimes even our actions. We are on autopilot. Think about driving home from work. Do you sometimes get home and realize you barely remember the drive home? This is a non-detrimental wakeful sleep. However, when our brains are in negative rumination cycles, it is harmful to our bodies and minds. Step one of getting above the line in our thinking is to become aware of when we have started destructively spinning in our own minds.

Our brains are wired to have the same thoughts over and over again, unless we intentionally change them. "Neurons that fire together, wire together" is a phrase that is commonly used to describe how our brain works. This phrase means that the thoughts we think tend to happen again and again in our minds, just like the metaphor of rain running down a hillside carving a path in the soil. Another great metaphor is the first time it snows on a hill: If we go sledding down a path, the next time we take our sled down, we usually go down the same path again. To make a new sledding path, we need to step away from the existing route and create a new one. Sometimes even when we do that our sled starts on the new path and then drifts right back to the old one. Our brains work the same way with thoughts. We need to be very intentional and aware to start changing our thought patterns to build more wellbeing and resiliency. We need to create new sledding paths in our minds.

It is important in the discussion of resiliency to create a distinction between our thoughts and our emotions. Sometimes we think resiliency means that we don't have emotions, or if we do, we try to change them. I want to be very clear that I am not asking you to change your emotions. Emotions are energy in motion. I like to think about emotions like waves in the ocean: some are big, some are small, and they change on a regular basis. Just like we would not try to block a wave in the ocean, I don't want you to block emotion. Emotions linger in the body when we do not give ourselves space to feel. Resiliency is about our mindset, above or below the line, not changing our emotional landscape. I encourage you to feel when emotions come, to give yourself permission to feel and allow emotions to pass through you like waves in the ocean. Allowing yourself the space and time to feel your emotions is good for your mental and physical wellbeing. While both mindset and emotions can impact one another, working with the model is about shifting our thinking and mindset to build resiliency.

When we think back to the definition of resiliency, it is the ability to recover quickly from difficulties. If we are recovering from something, we have to have a strong foundation to recover back to. If we do not have the capacity from the start to handle the situation we face, then resiliency doesn't mean anything and is not a possibility. Having a strong foundation to start with points back to all of the things we have discussed throughout this book in the context of wellbeing. Having a strong foundation in your Vital Leadership makes resiliency a true possibility. Resiliency also strengthens our capacity for others and expands our ability to be more Empathetic Leaders.

Like most things we have discussed, building resiliency takes practice. I would like for you to take a moment and practice with the worksheet below. In the center bar, I want you to think about a current situation, challenge, or change you are experiencing. Write it down. After you have identified the situation, write down where your mind goes when it travels below the line. It could be past or future or both. Once you have identified those thoughts, think about what positive thought patterns above the line would be. You can go in any quadrant, past or future or both. We can only become masters of our own mind if we build our awareness around the existing thought patterns that we tend to get stuck in. Here is one example to help you think through each quadrant:

Resiliency Worksheet Example

PAST		FUTURE
I learned from the last house I lost that I need to check the MLS every morning in case the right house gets listed.	Being Present	I am going to set some milestones to help us stay focused on getting the right house.
Purchasing a new home		
We lost the last two houses we bid on. If only I would have found that house sooner.	Stress / Rumination	We are never going to find the right house. What if there are no houses on the market that ever work for us?

Resiliency Worksheet

PAST	FUTURE
Being Present	
Stress	Rumination

To download a Resiliency Worksheet, visit www.connectedec.com/
brilliant-book.

"Stress is not what happens to us. It's our response to what happens. And response is something we can choose."

—Maureen Killoran

The first time I heard this quote, it honestly frustrated me. I had so many people in my life over the years tell me not to stress, and that really made no sense to me. When I was trying to get pregnant for the first time and struggling with miscarriages, people would say to me, "Don't stress; that will just make it harder to get pregnant." That caused me only to be stressed about being stressed. My thoughts had run away with me and I had no awareness of what not stressing meant. We often tell people, with the best of intentions, not to stress. However, that advice without a toolset and understanding of it only leads further in the wrong direction. I encourage you to utilize the Resiliency Worksheet for yourself, team members, and family to help build your capacity for awareness, a positive mindset and resiliency. Even how we view stress, either as a positive or a negative, can impact how we respond to it.

Stress researchers Alia Crum and Kelly McGonigal at Stanford University have been examining stress and mindsets for years. What they consistently find is that people who believe that stress is helpful and have a positive perspective on it are more satisfied in life, less depressed and more productive and happy at work, and have greater confidence that they can cope with life challenges. They find more meaning in the struggles of life (McGonigal 2015). Being resilient means we can recognize that life's pressures are occurring to help us grow, not tear us down.

There is no better fable that shows the importance of struggle than the story about a boy and a butterfly: Once there was a little boy on a walk with his grandfather in the forest. The little boy found a butterfly still in its cocoon struggling to break free. The little boy ran and grabbed a stick to cut the cocoon to allow the butterfly to escape. His grandfather quickly realized what his grandson was doing and stopped him. When the little boy protested that he was trying to help the butterfly, his grandfather explained that the butterfly needs to struggle. In fact, the butterfly's struggle to push its way through the tiny opening of the cocoon pushes the fluid out of its body and into its wings. Without the struggle, the butterfly would never, ever fly. The boy's good intentions would have actually hurt the butterfly. As you experience life, keep in mind that struggling is an important part of our growth. In fact, most often it is the struggle that causes you to develop your ability to fly. Our ability to see struggle with a positive mindset is what creates our greatest resiliency.

Cultivate Gratitude

As we discuss positive mindset, I want to share one of the most powerful tools for helping you get above the line and also building more positive thinking and energy. It is the tool of gratitude. Gratitude is thankful appreciation and seeing each moment as a gift. There has been a vast amount of research completed in the field of positive psychology showing that gratitude is one of the most effective ways to build our resiliency, a positive mindset, and overall wellbeing. This research has been conclusive that gratitude is strongly and consistently associated with greater happiness and the ability to have a positive mindset. Psychologist, researcher, and bestselling author Shawn Achor has made a career studying the science of happiness. "Scientifically, happiness is a choice," Achor says. He explains that research has shown you can rewire your brain to make yourself happy by practicing simple happiness exercises every day for three weeks. One of the most effective tools Achor shares for rewiring your brain is to write down three things you are grateful for every day. These statements do not need to be different every day or profound. They can be as simple as you are grateful to see the sun rise or grateful for your lunch. Achor's research on positive mindset, gratitude, and happiness is astounding. As he states, positive mindsets are a choice and people with this mindset have one of the greatest competitive advantages. People with positive mindsets experience 31 percent higher productivity, 37 percent higher sales, 3 times greater creativity, and 23 percent fewer fatigue symptoms. They are also up to ten times more engaged, 40 percent more likely to receive a promotion, and 39 percent more likely to live to age 94.

We all have the capacity to build our mindset for positive thinking.

Achor states, "Training your brain to be positive is not so different from training your muscles at the gym. Recent research on neuro-plasticity—the ability of the brain to change even in adulthood—reveals that as you develop new habits, you rewire the brain." Using the practice of gratitude will help create new pathways in your brain, making it easier to move above the line in your thinking no matter what you are facing in your life. The first step in cultivating a gratitude practice is to begin noticing and writing down what you are grateful for. You can do this in so many different ways and they all work—a journal, on your computer, create a gratitude jar that you drop notes into, or whatever modality works for your life. An incredibly impactful way to take this to the next level is to start sharing your gratitude with others. Send an email, text, or better yet, pick up the phone or talk to someone in person and share how grateful you are to them. Gratitude will help you feel more positive emotions, relish good experiences, improve your health, build your resiliency, and build even stronger relationships.

Brad decided to try a gratitude practice for himself and his team. He began each morning writing down three things he was grateful for every day. He challenged his team to do the same. Brad also decided to change his team meeting structure and begin each meeting with each person sharing a personal or professional gratitude statement. Brad realized that the energy and mindset on his team was starting to shift even after only three weeks of implementing this practice. He also noticed that he was connecting more authentically to himself, which enhanced his connection with others as well. Brad decided to begin this practice at home with his family as well. Jane, Julie, Kayla, and Brad created a gratitude jar in their home. Every day they would add one new gratitude statement to the jar. At the end of the week, they would read all the gratitude statements together. Brad always felt a special feeling of connection with his family after the weekly readings. The pressure and pace of change didn't slow down in in the lives of Brad and his family, but his ability to keep himself above the line in his thinking personally and professionally began to improve. Brad was starting to cultivate his capacity for a positive mindset and an understanding of his mind, and he was headed down the path to greater resiliency.

CHAPTER 7

Raise Your EQ (Emotional Intelligence) Through Mindful Leadership

One of the most emotionally charged and intense meetings Brad conducted every quarter was his leadership team's budget review meeting. During these meetings, Brad would do a deep dive into the financials of the business and required each of his direct reports to come ready to discuss performance metrics. I joined the meeting one quarter to see how Brad led these meetings and how his team responded to him. When I walked into the room, I could immediately feel the tension and anxiety. All eight of Brad's direct reports sat waiting in anticipation for the meeting to begin. His first leader reported the metrics with ease and Brad seemed patient and curious in his questions. I was happy to see that even though the tension seemed high, the meeting was going much better than I anticipated. Then his leader Sarah began to discuss her financials. Brad's demeanor and body language changed instantly. His questions were filled with a tone that was harsher and more direct. I could see his face was turning red and his body was agitated. Brad became reactive and not the leader I knew him to be. Sarah's body language changed too, and her shoulders started to roll forward. Her clarity at the beginning of the discussion vanished and she stumbled trying to explain her business. Sarah was a smart, articulate woman, but in that moment, she was unable to get her points across. What both Sarah and Brad didn't realize is that they were both in reactive states of mind and neither one was showing their best self. Brad's next step in his leadership journey was focusing on how to grow his Empathetic Leadership through becoming a mindful leader.

Throughout the last ten years, I have had an incredible mentor in the space of mindful leadership. Chad Herst has been a coach, business partner, and dear friend to me. Herst has been teaching mindfulness for over 20 years, and his insight and understanding of the mind-body connection and its impacts on leadership are profound. Our work together has informed my own leadership journey and the understanding of my own mind. Through my work with Herst and his coaching, I have become a more responsive, present person in all aspects of my life. Before becoming a mindful person, I was reactive to every issue I faced. While I might have faked it well on the outside, I was a mess on the inside. I felt like a duck: I was smooth on the surface, but internally and below the surface pedaling a million miles an hour. The study of mindfulness gave me access to a new choice: calm and peace.

The practices we have been discussing throughout this book, including resiliency and gratitude, are all elements of being a mindful leader and person. Mindful leadership is focused on cultivating self-awareness, wisdom, and self-mastery. A mindful leader is present in their leadership, communication, attention, and awareness of others. Mindfulness improves our abilities in the levels of Vital Leadership and is the foundation for Empathetic Leadership.

Over the last ten years, mindfulness has become a bit of a buzzword in business. We once thought being mindful was reserved for a life in isolation and required significant time every day. Advances in brain research through tools like an Electroencephalography (EEG),

Magnetic Resonance Imaging (MRI), and magnetoencephalography (MEG) have led us to understand the benefits of mindfulness as a practice for everyone. Before we discuss the neuroscience of mindfulness, let's talk about how our thoughts work.

One of the interesting lessons in my education as an executive coach was the work we did around understanding how thoughts work. The human mind is not linear in thinking patterns; it is like we have 100 people all talking to us at once. It is oftentimes hard to get clarity on what thoughts to follow and give energy to. When we have so many thoughts at once, we can't get to our deepest, most clear thoughts. Think about the metaphor of water for a moment. Herst teaches, "When water is choppy with lots of waves, you can't see past the surface. Our brains are very similar to that. We often are on the surface of our thoughts with little clarity, depth, or understanding that we actually are in control. Mindfulness is the ability to still the waters of our mind whenever we need to, so we can see into our deepest levels of thinking." Mindful leaders develop their self-awareness, emotional management, and resilience so that they can make more informed, better choices. Mindful leadership is accessed through the practice of mindfulness meditation.

Meditate to Access Mindful Leadership

Meditation trains the mind to pay attention mindfully. It's a practice that's designed to exercise the key elements: directing attention and opening awareness. As we discussed with mindset, meditation is a tool that trains the brain and is like gym for the mind. Most of us don't work out so that we can win strength competitions. We go to the gym so that we can be strong in life. Likewise, meditation is something we do so that we have the capacity to tap into mindful awareness when we need it.

Most people believe they are bad at meditation. People have the idea that when you meditate, your thoughts should literally be gone. That is actually impossible. Our brains are always going, and mindful meditation is not about eliminating our thoughts. Instead of stopping thought, meditation helps us clear away clutter, settle down, and find calm. Every day, we process more than 60,000 thoughts and a cavalcade of accompanying emotions. It is easy to understand how the mind can get disordered, confused, and overwhelmed with this constant flow of thoughts, feelings, and sensations. Herst teaches that mindful meditation is the practice of directing our attention to the present, getting distracted, and then redirecting our attention over and over again. We are developing the simple skill of returning to the present moment, not striving for the impossible feat of unwavering concentration. He explains, "It is also not an exercise in focus, even though you may actually grow your capacity for focus. Mindful meditation is about being an observer of your thoughts. The objective of mindfulness meditation is to pay attention to the present moment without judgment. It is not to turn off your mind."

I often hear and see people try meditation and decide it is not for them. Their experience is hard and feels bad, and the practice just isn't something they want to do. There are two main reasons I see this happen. First, people are trying to meditate for longer than needed, and second, the meditation becomes more like an exercise in self-abuse. A person will sit down for the first time and decide to meditate for 30 minutes. Within the first 30 seconds their thoughts sound something like this: "Has it been 10 minutes yet? "This is so hard," "I am really bad at this," "My mind is way too busy to do this," "I should have never tried this," "Why did I think I could do this?" "I am really not good at this." Of course, you won't enjoy the practice when all you are doing is thinking poorly of yourself. The first thing to change is your perception of this practice. There is no good and bad in meditation, it is simply the act of doing it. Like any new thing we do, meditation takes practice. The more you do it, the easier it will be. We need to be gentle and compassionate in our minds. I learned from Herst that learning to meditate is like training a puppy to sit. When you are teaching a puppy to sit, the puppy gets up over and over again. You gently and compassionately bring the puppy back to a sitting position to help him learn how to sit. Our minds are the same way; as your thoughts begin to run away from you, you can gently bring them back with attention and focus on your breath and the present moment. Begin your practice slowly with short-duration meditations. It is similar to when you begin physical exercise—don't overdo it.

Starting a meditation practice is a bit like taking up running. You'll have a much better experience and more success if you start small. You wouldn't run a marathon out of the gate, you'd start with a short run/walk to help condition your body. Likewise, don't start with a 30-minute meditation. You can get so much out of doing just 5 minutes a day and building the habit. It's much more valuable to do 5 minutes every day than 35 minutes once a week. When I start someone in a meditation practice, we start with just 1 minute a day with the intention to build up to 5 minutes.

If you practice mindfulness meditation for as little as 5 minutes per day, you'll enhance your ability to recognize your thoughts, feelings, sensations, and biases in the moment, not just when you are formally meditating. Although people have been practicing meditation for centuries and reporting benefit, science is now beginning to validate these experiences.

Just as regular physical movement changes the body, research is showing that mindfulness meditation actually changes the brain. A Harvard-led team at Massachusetts General Hospital studied participants in an 8-week mindfulness meditation program. The study showed that aside from the relaxation and stress-reduction benefits reported by the participants, the brain structure itself changed. Regions associated with memory, sense of self, empathy, and stress showed signs of strengthening.

Understand Your Brain

Our nervous system has two tracks. The sympathetic nervous system kicks the body into action to escape threats. The parasympathetic nervous system relaxes the body so it can rest and digest. Our brains were also designed to react to acute, life-threatening stress and then regain a sense of calm once the danger passes. The part of our brain that is responsible for our fight, flight, or freeze response is called the amygdala.

All physical and emotional threats are equally alarming to our brains and nervous system. Our mind and body react the same way whether we're facing a grizzly bear in our path, arguing with our spouse, or struggling under an overloaded schedule. Adrenaline and cortisol course through our blood, giving us a burst of energy. Our breath speeds up, and blood rushes away from our brain and into our heart and limbs. We don't think clearly in this state; we're meant to act faster than we can think. This state is called an amygdala hijack.

Learning to recognize when our brains are in amygdala hijack can save us from saying things we regret and acting in a reactive way. This self-awareness can help us to pause and take steps to calm ourselves before we act. Our feelings have the potential to be allies. The more sensitive we are at detecting the internal changes that can send us into amygdala hijack, the less reactive we become. Think about the last time you were cut off in traffic. What happened to your body? Did your heart race, face become warm, breathing speed up? Did you get tension in your shoulders, a jumpy sensation in your chest? Getting cut off in traffic should elicit this reaction. We are in physical danger speeding down a road. Our bodies are the first place to look to know when we are in this state. We will have a physical reaction first. This is also true when we face emotional stress. As we have discussed, our bodies do not know the difference between a physical and emotional stressor. Your body will show the same signs it does when you are cut off in traffic.

When we are in a state of hijack, our deepest level of thinking is cut off. The part of the brain that enables us to problem-solve, empathize, and enact nuanced responses based on our goals is called the prefrontal cortex. In order to turn this part of the brain back on, we need to calm our bodies to let our brains know we are not in physical danger. When our survival brain is in the lead, we fail to understand our present circumstances with clarity and end up reacting inappropriately and disproportionately. We need the prefrontal cortex online to be able to consider and choose our response.

Consider for a moment what reactivity often looks like in leadership. If we put up a fight, ultimately, we try to control a situation by doing whatever is necessary for our point of view to prevail, regardless of who gets hurt along the way. We rely on jokes, sarcasm, or snide remarks. We cut people off or change the subject. We say hurtful or insulting things, interrupt others, and will even resort to raising our voices if needed.

When we go into fight mode when our brain is in amygdala hijack, we tend toward control, and we can be sure that our teams will hold back on us. Employees that feel dictated to may be compliant, but they likely won't reveal what they honestly think. They'll obscure the facts and, instead, tell us what we want to hear. They won't be very committed to the outcome of whatever decisions we impose on them.

If we handle the situation with flight, while we do not necessarily run away, we avoid. We are afraid to be vulnerable, and instead, seek strength through self-reliance and independence. As a result, we put off interactions with people and situations that trouble us. We hold back from sharing our perspective on sensitive subjects. We don't offer constructive feedback because we don't want to deal with the drama that can result.

If we are in hijack mode, we are avoidant, and our teams will avoid sharing hard truths with us too. After all, we've proven to them time and again that we don't want to hear it. As a result, people tiptoe around us. This avoidance behavior can be so frustrating for some that it can create an environment where people feel alone in their inability to tell the truth. If they believe they have to keep it to themselves long enough, they will resort to either gossip or public outrage that can threaten our positions of leadership.

Reactivity undermines our leadership, teams, and organizations. To be a mindful leader means being responsive versus reactive. The greatest access back to our presence and responsiveness is actually through the breath. The easiest and most accessible way to stimulate the body's relaxation response is to take the diaphragmatic breath. When the brain and body have relaxed, we are back in the parasympathetic nervous system and prefrontal cortex and we have the calm we need to not only be responsive, but also to fully digest our food, sleep, connect with others, concentrate, solve complex problems, and create. We don't need to wait for calm to overtake us naturally when we are in a state of hijack; we can actually stimulate the relaxation response through our breath.

In order to utilize the breath successfully, we have to become aware of when we are actually in an amygdala hijack. This takes awareness of the body and mind. It is worthwhile to spend some time thinking about what triggers you, what your typical reactive response is, and what first signs your body gives you are?

Use Stop, Look, Go to Become Responsive

One of the most useful self-awareness tools that we share with our clients, developed by Chad Herst, is a mindful leadership model called Stop, Look, Go. Herst developed this model based on the work of Brother David Steindl-Rast, a Benedictine monk known for interfaith dialogue and his work on the interaction between spirituality and science. Brother David came up with a simple formula to help people access gratefulness, but Herst showed it works equally well as a practice of engaged mindfulness.

The formula includes three steps: Stop, Look, and Go. It's easy to remember because it uses the same steps we learned as children when crossing the street.

Stop: Brother David talks about how pausing puts us in touch with "the gift this moment offers." It's a beautiful image, finding a gift in the moment. But it is also a core tenant of mindfulness. Herst shares, "We stop to come back to the present moment and get in touch with our inner experience." As leaders, our days are typically filled with unceasing motion. We rarely take a break. We are full steam ahead and have been rewarded for being so. We pride ourselves on our ability to act swiftly. But when we are triggered, it's better to pause and give ourselves the power to create and respond appropriately. This can be difficult when our nervous system is primed, but this is a moment when it's especially important to stop and take that diaphragmatic breath. The simple act of pausing with the breath stimulates the prefrontal cortex, the portion of the brain that allows us to move through the world with wisdom, foresight, and level-headedness. It also naturally dampens amygdala activity.

Stopping does not need to take a lot of time. We can often stop an amygdala hijack in the time it takes us to take one deep breath.

Look: Brother David talks about how looking allows us to see "the opportunity available now." By first pausing and then looking, we can distinguish between the emotions we feel, the facts of the situation, and the outcomes we want. This allows us to tailor the most appropriate response. We look for the opportunity and appropriate action. Engaged mindfulness asks us to consider the results that we want to create. What impact do we want to have? What needs attention? What action is most appropriate? We go beyond noticing to formulate a response that bridges the gap between the present situation and our desired result. Looking, like stopping, does not require a great deal of time. Sometimes we only need to look briefly to see clearly.

Go: Instead of retreating to a cave for an endless series of "stop and look," Brother David encourages us "to do something with this precious opportunity." When we are clear, we act. This is what makes Brother David's recipe distinct from most contemplative practices. When we engage, we give ourselves complete permission to follow the clarity that emerged in the "Look" phase. Mindful action does not mean that we always speak in soft, whispering tones. When we are engaged in a mindful way, we bring whatever energy is needed for a given situation. Sometimes we must take strong and forceful action, but we make a choice to do what needs to be done rather than react unconsciously to our emotions. By recognizing our emotions and responding from a calm and centered state of mind, we improve our chances for a positive outcome. Beware of getting stuck in the "Look" phase and giving too much weight to having a plan. Sometimes we just need to pick up a foot, move it forward, and take the step that's in front of us. At these moments, we must summon our courage so we can act in spite of being afraid and not knowing the outcome. When we take the first step, it's not the end of our journey. It returns us back to the start of Brother David's model. We stop and look to notice our impact. This model is a circular model and can be repeated over and over again, even in a single conversation.

Herst teaches that practicing mindfulness meditation helps us develop an innate capacity to pause before we act, especially when we feel strong negative emotion. It gives us an opening to break free of our autopilot-like ingrained behaviors and gives us more capacity for choice. The Harvard study I mentioned earlier in this chapter actually found through neuroimaging that the participants' brains physically changed after just eight weeks of meditation. The prefrontal cortex grew and the amygdala shrank in size. That is with only 5 minutes a day.

There is evidence that mindfulness practice can actually rewire your brain so that the amygdala is less reactive. In a study at the Psychiatric Neuroimaging Research Program at Massachusetts General Hospital, fMRIs were used to assess cortical thickness in 20 participants with extensive mindfulness meditation experience. The middle prefrontal cortex was thicker in mindfulness participants than matched controls. Because mindfulness practice activates neural firing of the prefrontal cortex, this brain structure, in turn, produces proteins that thicken it, thus strengthening it.

Similar to the Harvard study, Massachusetts General Hospital discovered that the density of the amygdala decreased after eight weeks of mindfulness meditation training, limiting the reactive nature of the amygdala. With a smaller amygdala, we reduce the likelihood of an amygdala hijack and increase the probability that the prefrontal cortex can step in to provide an appropriate and nuanced response. Another study conducted by Julie Brefcyznski-Lewis revealed that when long-term meditators were subjected to disturbing sounds, like a woman screaming, they showed less amygdala activation compared to novice meditators. The long-term meditators were able to process the sounds, but did not have an emotional reaction to the disturbance and could stay in the prefrontal cortex of the brain. The more hours a person meditated, the lower the activation. This and the data above provide structural evidence for brain plasticity associated with mindfulness practice.

Over days, months, and years of mindfulness meditation practice, we become more present and less reactive. We develop a wakefulness about what's going on inside and outside of ourselves. We can learn to pause, notice our reactivity, wait for the intensity of emotion to pass, and then respond in a way that can affect the situation constructively. When we become familiar with our own patterns of emotional reactivity, we are not thrown off track as easily. Essentially, we're training ourselves to not get triggered, to stay present in emotionally charged situations, and to stop obsessively attempting to change external situations to calm our internal reactivity. Mindfulness is a process of staying present and slowly dissolving the reactivity that we carry with us. Once dissolved, we can work with people and situations on a deeper, more connected level.

Start a Mindful Meditation Practice

Meditation is a practice and you will reap rewards with consistency. Five minutes every day is more useful than 30 minutes one or two days a week. Starting with 1 minute a day is a great way to start to cultivate the habit.

Place: Anywhere you can sit easily with minimal disturbance: a corner of your bedroom or any other quiet spot in your home or office. (It can even be in your seat on a flight.) A peaceful environment will support your efforts.

Posture: You can meditate while lying down, but it's easy to fall asleep that way. As you are trying to expand awareness, we recommend that you start with a seated posture. Find a posture on the chair or cushion in which you can easily sit erect but relaxed in good posture without being uncomfortable for the duration of your practice.

Notice: Before you begin, get a sense of how you feel physically. Take note of your mood and state of mind. There is no preferable state to start meditation. Take a moment and be here. Observe the breath: Our breathing always occurs in the present moment. This is why it makes a good focus for meditation.

Tools: There are several great apps available for download to support a meditation practice. My favorite one is Insight Timer. This app has meditation teachers from all over the world that can lead you in guided meditation or a timer if you prefer to just focus on your breath.

Grow Your Emotional Intelligence

Emotional Intelligence is the capacity to effectively recognize our own feelings, the feelings of others, and our situations. During the budget meeting I had observed with Brad, it was clear that he was not tapped into his own feelings or how Sarah was feeling during their difficult interaction. Brad and I debriefed after the meeting together. I shared my observations and asked him if he noticed the change in his body language, tone, and questioning. I also wondered if he realized how similar the situation was to how his board president, Jeff, reacted to him before our coaching together. Brad shared with me that he always felt triggered by Sarah. Her numbers were down for the year and he didn't think she had a good enough handle on it. After a lot of questions about the situation I got to the bottom of what Brad was feeling. He told me that he felt like he was failing her as a leader. When she wasn't clear with him, he was triggered because it brought him back to feelings of failing as a parent as well. As we began to uncover what was under the surface, Brad started to realize how his reactiveness was not only hurting Sarah's ability to respond, it was also stifling her leadership, the exact opposite of what Brad was trying to do. Sarah was also in a reactive state as well and was freezing during Brad's questions. I shared with Brad how his emotions and reaction were impacting Sarah, the team, and the energy in the room. He agreed to start utilizing "Stop, Look, Go" and being more observant of his emotional landscape as well as others. What Brad and I were working on was his competence in emotional intelligence.

Leaders with high emotional intelligence (EQ) can recognize and adapt quickly to the emotions and situations they are in. Mindful leadership gives us our greatest window and access into our emotional intelligence. A practice of mindfulness meditation is the number one way to build our emotional intelligence as a leader. Meditation strengthens the mind in awareness, responsiveness, emotional control, and resiliency, which all enable emotional intelligence and effective leadership to take place. The ability to manage your emotions and remain calm under pressure has a direct link to your performance. TalentSmart, authors of *Emotional Intelligence 2.0,* conducted research with more than a million people, and found that 90 percent of top performers in their fields are skilled at managing their emotions in times of stress in order to remain calm and in control. Leading emotional intelligence author and expert Daniel Goleman reports from studying competency tests across 188 companies that EQ is twice as important for predicting success as IQ or technical skills.

One of the main reasons that EQ is so critical in leadership is the fact that emotions are truly contagious. Herst explains, "Humans are wired to mirror one another in emotion, language, and posture. When mirror neurons fire, they trick our limbic brains into feeling emotions similar to those of the people around us." For example, if someone is angry and stressed, others around him or her unconsciously mirror their facial expressions and end up feeling angry and stressed as well. This mirroring is what creates emotional contagion, which is defined as the tendency for two or more individuals to emotionally converge. The stronger the emotion, the more it spreads, thus affecting others.

Even the stress hormone cortisol is contagious. When the body and mind are stressed, cortisol is excreted through the skin and can by absorbed by others in close proximity. You might say that cortisol lives in a cloud around us. Just being around someone who is stressed, you can become stressed yourself. As a leader, people are watching you all of the time. In fact, people are twice as likely to mirror you than anyone else in the room. It is essential as leaders that we work on our EQ continually.

Many people believe that as our leadership roles expand, we naturally move higher on the EQ scale. Unfortunately, this is exactly the opposite of what happens. According to research conducted by TalentSmart, our EQ scores peak at the manager level and gradually go down, with the lowest scores at the C-suite level. Responsibilities, meetings, and pressures increase as leadership roles grow, leaving a potential gap in EQ. If we want to expand our capabilities in the EQ space, we need to be intentional. Mindful meditation is the number one way to develop our EQ capabilities.

According to Peerayuth Charoensukmongkol (2015) in his paper "Benefits of Mindfulness Meditation on Emotional Intelligence,

General Self-Efficacy, and Perceived Stress," mindfulness meditation helps grow emotional intelligence in these ways:

- It improves your ability to comprehend your own emotions.

- It helps you learn how to recognize the emotions of other people around you.

- It strengthens your ability to govern and control your emotions.

- It improves your ability to use emotions effectively through determining which emotions are beneficial for certain activities.

Utilize Mindful Listening to Access Your EQ

When we focus our whole attention on the person with whom we're communicating, we are listening with curiosity—utilizing the two-dimensional listening tool. Mindful listening is another term for two-dimensional listening. When we are truly present with another person and aware of their emotions, we can tap into our own self-awareness and emotional intelligence at a deeper level. When we are mindfully listening to a person, we are not only hearing the words they are saying, we are tuned into their body language, tone, and emotions. We pay attention to the details of what they are saying instead of just waiting for our turn to respond. We often believe our role and value as leaders and parents is to solve problems. This is not the case. Human beings have a fundamental need to be seen, heard, and acknowledged. Mindful listening creates the opportunity for a person to truly hear another person, rather than respond with the answer or a solution.

One of the greatest gifts we can give to people around us is to mindfully listen. Mindful listening is not only a tool that expands our EQ, it is also the greatest connection tool we have. As executive coaches, we spend the majority of our day in mindful listening when working with our clients. Our job is to stay in curiosity and help reflect our client's wisdom back to them. True change comes from within and we, as coaches, simply create the space for our clients to do this. Next time you want to help someone grow, try using your mindful listening tools to help them see their own path versus telling them the way. You will be amazed not only at the person's ability to take action, but also the deep connection that is present through your listening and the space you create.

Brad decided to sit down with Sarah to talk about how they could both be more responsive versus reactive with one another. I asked Brad to lean into his mindful listening tools to help her in her leadership growth. Brad was able to stay present and curious in the conversation. Sarah shared with him how disappointed she was in how she kept performing in the budget review meetings. She actually knew the answers to his questions and had the data, but she was never able to access it. Brad shared with her the work we had been doing around his emotional reactivity and he promised to show up differently in their next meeting. They both agreed to breathe more, stay calm with one another, and pause if they went in a direction that wasn't healthy. I attended the next quarterly budget meeting. Brad and Sarah stayed true to the commitments they made to one another. Their leadership and connection with one another was truly different. Sarah and Brad showed up in their best selves and both stayed responsive with one another. It was a joy for me to see.

To get started in being a mindful listener, I want you to practice these simple steps. First, make sure you are free from distractions when in the conversation. As you engage with another person, tap into your childlike curiosity for them. Focus on the person in front of you as much as possible. Try to ask only simple questions that start with "What" or "How." Stay away from using the word "Why." Surprisingly, when we start a question with "Why" it naturally makes the other person defensive. For example, think about these two questions: "Why do you like that sweater?" versus "What do you like about that sweater?" The "Why" question makes you defend your liking of the sweater, where the "What" question opens a conversation about you and what you like. Try not to get stuck in thinking about questions, and instead keep your curiosity open. At any time, you may use the prompt, "Tell me more." You will be amazed at the depth of conversation and connection you will have by using these tools. Mindful listening is a key not only to connection and EQ, but it is also an incredible way to learn how we get in our own way when we are trying to grow to be our best.

PART IV

Embodying Visionary Leadership

CHAPTER 8

Break Through Barriers in Your Mind to Lead with Real Power

Brad called me in a panic. We had been working together for nine months at this point, and it was the first time I had heard real fear in his voice. He asked if we could meet right away. That afternoon I met him at his office and asked, "Brad, I have never heard such concern in your voice, what is going on?"

Brad shared that he just got the tap on the shoulder we were hoping he would get. Brad was asked to take the CEO role starting in a couple of months. Yes! This was everything Brad had been working so hard for. Now Brad was facing his inner critic. In this moment, the message he was hearing in his mind was that he wasn't enough to be truly successful in this new role. Brad's fear had taken over. It was time for him to step into his power and become the Visionary Leader he dreamed of being, but we had some work to do. Brad had to distinguish between his self-critic voice and his true best self.

The self-critic or inner critic, also called the saboteur, is a part of the human experience. It is that voice in our minds that is hyper-critical, and it tends to become particularly noisy in times of change. This voice creates an echo chamber where the self-judging, shaming,

belittling, and fault-finding are too deafening to allow us to see ourselves, our opportunities, or the problem clearly. Surprisingly, it is in
every person, no matter what position you have, what success you
have achieved, or how old you are. We all have the saboteur voice.
I have worked with clients considered successful by all external
measures: CEOs, entrepreneurs, rising stars. I have yet to encounter
anyone without an inner critic. Understanding the inner critic expands our awareness of self in Vital Leadership. It also expands our
awareness of others through Empathetic Leadership. And, knowing
how to work with the voice of our inner critic allows us to embrace
the true power of Visionary Leadership.

Time and time again I have been asked if I have conquered my
saboteur because I am a coach. The answer is no. In fact, there is no
conquering involved in working with our saboteurs. There is awareness, acceptance, and love that help transform our relationship with
this part of ourselves. I am always learning, growing, and finding
new ways to work with this side of myself. The truth is, my saboteur
almost prevented me from writing this book. I spent years telling
myself that I wasn't a writer and that I could never write a book. My
saboteur had a big story—I was a speaker, not a writer. I am dyslexic
and had been telling myself this story since I was a kid. I was lucky
enough to work with an incredible coach in writing this book,
Catherine Gregory, who quickly spotted my saboteur and helped me
reconnect to my best self. Catherine helped me see how writing this
book was possible, gently bringing awareness to the saboteur voices
getting in the way. She guided me to take action from my wisest self
instead of focusing my energy on my saboteur. We all have this voice
and our power comes from learning to work with it, not against it.

Understanding the Saboteur in Times of Change

Any time we move from the known to the unknown, we encounter
our saboteur voice or voices. For a moment, think about growth,

learning, and transition. In order to do any of these things, we have to pass through what is comfortable, what we know, to the unknown. This is your edge. You have probably heard the quote, "Life begins at the edge of your comfort zone." The reason being on the edge of your comfort zone is so difficult is because the saboteur is often the loudest in these moments. Transition requires that we cultivate awareness of our inner critic to move through change and growth successfully.

Our brains are wired to have the saboteur voice. The inner critic actually develops at a young age, usually by age 5, and is a part of our neurobiology to keep us safe and out of danger. Our primitive brains are wired to keep us out of physical danger. Since our brains can't distinguish physical from emotional danger, the saboteur gets very loud in times of change or discomfort. The motivation of the inner critic is to keep us safe in the familiar. The saboteur traps us in situations or patterns that are not healthy.

My work with Chad Herst illuminated the wisdom of working with the saboteur. "It's important to understand that your inner critic has a positive intent," says Herst. "This may seem counterintuitive given the way it attacks you, but its objective is to protect you from pain. It employs criticism believing that if we could be more successful, thinner, stronger, smarter, more perfect, or if we could get that next job, we wouldn't be rejected or hurt. If we corrected what we deem to be weak, imperfect, and unlovable about ourselves, we would fit in and stop feeling like such an outsider. The inner critic believes its harsh and negative attacks will improve our lives."

The saboteur uses words like "should" and language that lacks compassion. The voice of the saboteur can take on many different messages for different people; however, it is always the voice that gets in the way of us reaching our greatest potential. We have many different saboteur voices in our minds and the work we must do as leaders is get clear on the distinction between our inner critic and our best selves. We have a choice as to what thoughts we give our energy to. The first step is to recognize what your common saboteur voices sound like and how they are getting in your way.

Working with Our Perfectionism

In my work with executives, it's rare that I see someone who doesn't have some measure of a perfectionist saboteur. The people I work with typically hold themselves to a superhuman standard of perfection. They privately worry whether they are deserving of their success and status. They fear that it could all disappear in a moment, that they could be "found out," and that they might have little worth beyond their achievements. This is sometimes labeled "the imposter syndrome."

When Brad and I talked about the CEO role, he shared his fear that he was not capable enough and that the board would find it out. Brad's fear couldn't have been further from the truth. He not only had the business acumen, he had the vision the organization needed, the people strategy, and the overall leadership to help take his company to the next level. His perfectionist saboteur was terrified of failing and not being good enough. Brad's perfectionist saboteur came into existence at a young age and had created a continual pattern of behavior throughout his career. Brad and I had discussed in depth some of the ways this saboteur had held him back in his life. We discovered in our work together that Brad had defined himself too often by others' definition of success and not his own. He had been driven time and time again to achieve to prove his value and worth without believing he was enough. Brad shared with me that when he took on his current role as president, he put everything into proving his value at the expense of everything else, including his health and happiness. He drove hard to show results and was more driven by fear and insecurity than his best self. As Brad stepped into his new CEO role, it was essential that he begin with his best self, not his perfectionist saboteur.

Fear of failure and perfectionism often compel executives to work harder than most. They are ambitious and can accomplish extraordinary feats. However, when the perfectionistic inner critic is fueling ambition, the result is punishing. Nothing is ever good enough. Achievement isn't something to be enjoyed; it's a way to measure our worth and there's always someone who has accomplished more or better. Like all forms of shame, there are two problems with perfectionism: It saddles us with persistent feelings of inadequacy and it serves to alienate us. While achievement is not a bad thing, it is important we are achieving for the right reasons and not sacrificing our own fulfillment in the process. When we hold ourselves to superhuman standards, we can cut ourselves off from self-compassion and joy. We may play it safe rather than stretch ourselves out of a fear of failures. When we do fail, it can be harder to get back up. We may hold others to the same impossible standards, creating resentment and distrust.

The reality is that we are all human. And humans are a combination of brilliance and shadow, vulnerability, and strength. We are neither one nor the other. Brené Brown, research professor, speaker, and bestselling author shares, "Only when we are brave enough to explore the darkness will we discover the infinite power of our light." For people who have been so successful, self-compassion for our entire selves can be elusive. It requires that we accept our humanity and see that we are no worse or better than anyone else. That we, like all beings, deserve unconditional kindness. When we can love our full selves, including the parts of ourselves we are not as proud of, that is when we can access our greatest potential. The more we can love our darkest parts, the greater we can shine our brightest light.

Cultivate Self-Compassion

The key to working with our inner critic is love and compassion. Imagine for a moment if you had a friend that treated you the way you treat yourself. Would you still want that friend in your life? In order to work with our inner critic, we must learn to treat our entire selves with kindness. One of the best ways to think of your saboteur is like a young child. The saboteur voice really has a child's understanding of the world around them. Our saboteur voices are developed at a young age and often these messages do not mature with us as we grow into adults. For a moment, think about Brad and the saboteur voice that was coming up for him. His inner critic said, "You are not good enough for this job and you are going to fail!" Many people think in order for Brad to not act on this voice, he should ignore it or shut it down. Trying to ignore the inner critic, fight it, or drown it out is an exercise in futility. This part of our brain is strong and fierce. The saboteur is part of our primitive wiring, which makes it a deep-seated part of us. The more you resist it, the more virulent it will become and the harder it will be for you to regain your connection to your best self. What Brad can do is acknowledge this voice by bringing his awareness to it, and give it understanding, reassurance, and compassion to let this part of himself feel more comfortable in the change. Using curiosity is a great way to bring awareness and kindness to this voice. Applying curiosity, Brad might ask, what is the inner critic trying to share with me? What judgment is my inner critic feeling? What does this experience feel like for my inner critic? How is my inner critic trying to protect me?

When we view this childlike part of our brain with understanding, compassion, and kindness we treat our whole selves with the love and respect we deserve as human beings. Our saboteurs are just as much a gift in our lives as any other part of our brains. Think for a moment how your saboteur voice has served you over the years. Brad's perfectionist saboteur helped him be prepared throughout his career for every opportunity put in front of him. Our saboteurs are not wrong or bad. They are a part of us. The work is to get clear on the voice and the message, to treat it with self-compassion, and know how to take action that is aligned with our best self, not our saboteur voice. When we can recognize the inner critic, it allows us as leaders to move into change professionally and personally with more ease and ability. While we rarely talk about this topic in Corporate America, we should. We all face some version of the inner critic and we would be well-served by sharing our experiences with one another. The truth is, nobody connects with our perfectionism; they connect with our humanity.

Brad and I spent time exploring the voice of his perfectionist saboteur and how it was showing up with this new opportunity. We gave his saboteur space, compassion, awareness, and understanding in our conversation and helped that part of himself feel seen and heard. Brad started to see how listening to his saboteur voice in his new role would ultimately land him right back where we started our work together: a place of burnout. He knew it was time to take action from the part of himself we had been focused on, his best self. We went back and reconnected to his vision statement. Brad wanted to be a vibrant leader and father that guided people, including his daughters, to their highest potential. In order to fulfill his vision to be the leader, father, and husband he wanted to be, he would need to continue to lean into the work we had done in every aspect of his life. He would have to continue his focus on his energy, wellbeing, mind, body, and spirit. Brad would need to continually take action from his vision, values, and best self, while at the same time giving his saboteur voice compassion throughout the change.

Stepping into Change, One Small Step at a Time

When we learn to work with the barriers our own mind creates with our saboteurs in the face of change, we can begin to take the steps forward toward our best selves. We can be aware of the discomfort that will arise and work with our inner critic successfully during these times. Real transformative change does not happen by turning our lives upside down. Real change happens one small, achievable step at a time. In order to create the change we desire, we need to cultivate new actions and habits to support the change we want to see in our lives. Over the last 30 years there has been incredible progress made in the understanding of how our brains work to create new habits in our lives. The research shows that to create real, measurable change, we need to start with something called a "keystone habit." A keystone habit is a small, attainable change you can make in your life that feels easy. This keystone habit is the launch point to make the next small change and then the next small change. As leaders, we have a lot on our plates. What often happens is we decide to make a change that is large in scale and when we don't stick to it, we go into a cycle of self-abuse. Our saboteur takes over, making us wrong, bad, and not enough. Our saboteur voice increases our stress, which ends up perpetuating the behaviors we are trying to move away from. I want you to let go of the old model, that change happens in large increments. Small, incremental changes are what lead to great transformative change.

Life is full of ups and downs. Sometimes we feel deeply connected with our best selves and sometimes we feel at a really low point. Our leadership and wellbeing are a journey, not a destination. You will hit bumps in the road on this journey. There will be weeks where you are traveling, or there is more on your plate, or your personal life may have strain. It is important during these times that you become aware you are in a dip and not let your saboteur take over, because your saboteur will take you deeper and deeper into that dip. When you see that you are in a dip, that you have fallen, simply get back up and take one small step forward in the direction of your best self. This is the time to lean on a keystone habit to begin the process of getting connected again. The picture below shows the ups and downs in life that we all face.

The curved line is life. We have ups and down in our wellbeing, leadership, and life. When we are at the larger X, that is the time to think about the small step in front of you to begin the journey back to your best.

Let's spend some time finding a keystone habit that could work for you. Think about all of the things we have discussed in this book and go back to Chapter 1, where you created your energy recharge map. What is one small, achievable step you can take starting today? Found it? That is where I want you to start. If for any reason that step doesn't lead you toward change and your best self, be playful and try something else. Think about children for a moment. When a child is learning to walk, and falls down, do they berate themselves and say they will never learn to walk? Of course not. They simply get back up and try again. I ask you to take a step with that childlike, playful intention.

Our brains respond incredibly well to positive feedback loops. We are wired for making changes when we get some form of positive feedback. Positive feedback loops enhance and amplify the changes we are trying to make. Positive feedback helps our keystone habits really stick for the long term. In Charles Duhigg's best-selling book, *The Power of Habit*, he explains that habits have three important pieces: the trigger that initiates the behavior; the routine itself or the action you take; and finally, the reward that is the benefit you gain from doing the behavior. Behavioral psychology researchers have proven over and over again that this three-step habit structure is the way to cultivate good habits and break old ones. In thinking about your keystone habit, do not think only about the action itself. Think about what will initiate your habit and what positive reward you will receive from doing it. The positive feedback can be anything from a person you share with, a reward you give yourself, or an automated tracking system. For example, if I want to start a new habit of working out in the morning, I need to break this habit down into the trigger, routine, and reward. The trigger may be that I am going to set my clothes out the night before, or a more basic trigger could be an alarm that goes off loudly at 5 a.m. I could even put my alarm clock across the room to ensure I have to get out of bed to turn it off. The routine will entail getting dressed and heading to the gym, doing my workout, and then coming home. My reward could be a massage after a consistent month of working out or a simpler reward every day of a warm cup of coffee and a healthy breakfast after my workout.

Keep in mind that it is much easier to add something into your life first rather than stop a behavior you don't want. For example, when you focus on fueling your leadership with nutrition, it is better to add more healthy food into your nutrition than restrict yourself from something that is not healthy. The same is true in life; it is easier to add behaviors we want before stopping a behavior that is not serving our best self. When thinking about your keystone habit, try to think of it as an additive process. As you begin to define that keystone habit, it is important to recognize how that habit supports your overarching goals. One of the most important habits in my life is my morning routine. I have found in order to be the best wife, parent, and coach in my life, I need to spend my mornings pouring energy into myself. This entails waking up at 5 a.m., meditating, doing yoga, and heading to the gym with my CrossFit community. I come home and have my healthy breakfast and delicious coffee. I am nourished before my kids even wake up. This daily practice gives me the ability to show up at my best for everyone in my life. Without this routine, it would be incredibly hard for me to live my vision.

The Power of Intention

You have already connected to your best self in our visualization. You've thought about having accomplished all of the leadership and wellbeing goals you ever dreamed possible. In order to accomplish your goals, we need to get clarity on what they are. The power of intention is incredible. When you put out into the world what you are trying to do, magic happens. At the beginning of my work with clients, we get really clear on the goals we have for their leadership and life. I am always amazed at how the process of writing these goals down sets them in motion. This is the power of intention.

We know this to be true in business. We create organizational goals constantly, but when do we create the goals of our lives? I want you to start now. I invite you to spend some time thinking about the areas of the book we have discussed: leadership, nutrition, embodiment, resiliency, mindset, mindfulness, and breaking through barriers. First, create a goal for your best self. What is it that you want to accomplish, both professionally and personally? Then write down the supporting actions/habits you need to cultivate to make this goal a possibility. Next, what tools will support you? Perhaps there is a tool in this book or one you know about from your previous learning. Write down any tools you can use to support you. Support is next: Who or what do you need to support you to accomplish your goals? Write down anyone or anything that can support you through the process of accomplishing your goal. And finally, how will you measure whether you accomplish this goal? Make sure you don't skip the measurement step. This is important not only for the goal itself, but also to create a positive feedback loop that is essential for change. Below are both an example and a blank table to practice creating goals.

Goal-Setting Example

Category	Empathetic Leadership
Goal	I want my direct reports to feel really listened to during our one-on-one meetings.
Action(s)/Habit(s)	I will utilize mindful listening during our meetings, always turn my phone to silent, close my computer, and pay attention to my body language during these meetings.
Tool(s)	Mindful listening.
Support	I will share my goal with my direct reports and let them each know I am working on improving in this area of my leadership.
Measurement/ Feedback	I will ask for feedback at the end of each meeting.

Goal Setting Worksheet

Category	
Goal	
Action(s)/Habit(s)	
Tool(s)	
Support	
Measurement/Positive Feedback	

To download a Goal Setting Worksheet visit www.connectedec. com/brilliant-book.

Brad was feeling ready for his new opportunity. Many people believe that courage is the absence of fear. The real meaning of courage is having the fear and being willing to do it anyway. Brad was going to be courageous and step into the CEO role in the new year. The truth is, when we planned out his goals at the beginning of our work together, this was first on his list of professional goals. Brad had intentionally worked hard for the CEO job. He had spent our time together preparing his mind, body, and leadership for this opportunity. It was here and it was time for Brad to take on this role and put into action all that he had learned. Brad knew that creating a culture of leadership connected with wellbeing was something he wanted to do as the new CEO.

CHAPTER 9

Create a Community and Work Culture that Shines

Brad began his new role as CEO almost exactly one year after we began working together. Brad felt ready, in every aspect of his life, to take on this new challenge. He also knew that in order to live his vision and achieve the organization's highest potential, he would have to cultivate more connection throughout the company. This was the time for him to embody his roles as both a Vital and Empathetic Leader so that he could step into his real power as a Visionary Leader.

Human beings are meant to live in connection and community. We thrive through the relationships we cultivate, the people we love, and communities we are a part of. We are wired for emotional connection. Corporate America is a place of business and it is a community of people that are connected. Support systems can create a beautiful opportunity for accountability, collaboration, vulnerability, and transformation. Change happens when we are in communities of support. Dr. Ornish's work with people who had undergone heart bypass surgery showed that people were able to make significant lifestyle changes when they envisioned possibility and when they had the support of other people. Leveraging our existing networks and communities, in and out of the workplace, is essential to helping transform our leadership, wellbeing, and lives to truly become Visionary Leaders.

Find Your Tribe

You need support too. Being at the top is lonely and it is challenging. You are human and I hope you have learned through this book that your humanness is what makes you great. Leaders often try to keep everything together around them and rarely reach out to the people who deeply want to support them. We hold the flawed assumption that people will only respect us if we are invulnerable. We worry that we will lose respect if we show our humanity: failures, weaknesses, and emotions. Yet over the long haul, denying and hiding our humanity holds us back and undermines our ability to connect with people and get the support to create the changes we desire in our lives. It's lonely for us and it alienates the people who we need on our side. Often those around us can see when we are struggling and they want to help. Let the people who love you be your rock as you transform your life and leadership to the next level. Expert vulnerability researcher Brené Brown shares, "Courage starts with showing up and letting ourselves be seen."

Time and time again when I see leaders choose to open up to their friends, family, and colleagues and share their development goals, the first reaction they get is unwavering support. While it can feel vulnerable, this openness builds trust, connection, and accountability partners. The courage to share your vulnerabilities is a strength. It displays a confidence in your relationships and your ability to learn from your experiences. It acknowledges that you are human and that the people around you are valued and important to you. It demonstrates that you want their input and help. When you share with others, you will see that the people in your life will see you as strong, courageous, and a role model for actively focusing on your growth. It also creates permission for others to be open about their journey and development goals.

Cultivate a Movement

When you transform your leadership and life as a leader, you then have the ability to take your organization on the journey with you. You have the influence and power to cultivate a company culture and environment that lives out the core values we have discussed throughout this book; leadership and wellbeing can no longer be separate topics. A beautiful example of a CEO living and leading with these values is the CEO of Aetna, Mark Bertolini.

In an effort to reshape the culture of Aetna, Bertolini began offering wellness-focused classes after his own near-death experience and transformation. Aetna now offers classes in meditation and yoga. More than one-quarter of the company's workforce of 50,000 has participated in at least one class. Those who have participated report, on average, a 28 percent reduction in their stress levels, a 20 percent improvement in sleep quality, and a 19 percent reduction in pain. They have become more effective on the job, each gaining an average of 62 minutes per week of productivity, which Aetna estimates is worth $3,000 per employee per year. Creating and living a culture of leadership wellbeing is good for our business communities and for the bottom line.

First and foremost, it starts with you. You are a role model for how to be at the top and still take care of yourself physically, mentally, and emotionally. Managing personal wellbeing has the power to be a catalyst for positive change to your company's entire workforce. There is no more powerful support for any strategy than to lead by example. The best way to create and lead a successful wellbeing culture in any organization is for its leaders to model healthy behaviors. It's more about the "walk" than the "talk."

Your transformation as a leader and connecting the dots to wellbeing has incredible power when you share it and share it often. As the leader, if you can openly share your journey, you give others permission and inspiration to start on their journey. You create an environment of psychological safety and support. Through leading by example and voicing your belief in the importance of leadership and wellbeing, you can create a culture where people know they are valued and that they matter. Supporting others in their journey to wellbeing shows you care at the deepest levels. Full engagement in an organization happens when people feel seen and cared for. As you share your vulnerability, journey, and courage, you build your Visionary Leadership and inspire entire organizations to shine brightly. Your personal and professional alignment and your ultimate fulfillment serves as a tenfold magnifier in your Visionary Leadership.

Living into Your Fulfillment

There is a beautiful quote by an unknown author that states, "Purpose is discovering your gifts; fulfillment is giving them to the world." Fulfillment can be defined as a feeling of contentment or internal peace from doing what you intended to do in life. Fulfillment does not mean that you live in a state of bliss or that you don't wrestle with doubts or difficult emotions. People who are fulfilled experience the full range of human emotions and experiences, including sadness and setbacks. You can feel fulfilled and sad in the same moment.

Fulfillment is a state of being that comes from making a meaningful impact on the lives of others. It requires that you feel a sense of purpose and act in alignment with your own personal values. Meaning, like beauty, is in the eye of the beholder. It's you who must find the source of your meaning.

Brad had found his purpose, values, and alignment, and was in a true state of fulfillment as he started his CEO role. His relationships within the organization had become authentic, transparent, and connected. Brad brought his entire self to the role and was willing to share his vulnerability on a regular basis. He felt connected to his best self and those around him saw it too. In my follow up 360-leadership assessment for Brad, his team shared how excited they were for Brad's new role and how transformative the last year had been. The team, through Brad's leadership, had reached new heights of achievement and, more importantly, connection. Each team member felt enrolled in Brad's growth and knew they had been a part of it. Brad's willingness to share his journey and fulfillment inspired everyone around him to reach new heights. Brad was deeply proud of all of his growth at work, but more importantly he was proud of how he transformed his relationships at home. Kayla and Julie were closer to Brad now than they had ever been. They regularly opened up about their days and requested to spend one-on-one time with Brad. Brad finally felt like he was showing up as the father he wanted to be. Jane, his wife, also felt like she had her husband back. Brad had the energy for their girls and for her. They spent time again doing things they loved together and Jane even started biking with him on the weekends. The quality of their time had transformed over the last year. Brad felt personally and professionally aligned and fulfilled.

To be truly fulfilled you must feel a connection with something larger than yourself. That larger thing can be humanity or the earth or the generations that will follow you or people of a specific community or a spiritual tradition. It's rooted in a belief that you belong somewhere and serve a higher calling than self-gratification. Fulfillment is a matter of the spirit—that spark inside all of us—but it doesn't require that you hold any religious belief at all.

Fulfillment is a force multiplier for leaders. When we have clarity about our unique gifts for the world and act in alignment with our values, we have greater access to our highest levels of leadership. We are more inspiring and our energy is infectious. People can tell when a leader is fully engaged and impassioned in life. Fulfilled leaders know what they have to give and why there are here. They have a sense of meaning and purpose that applies to all aspects of their lives: family, community, and work. Fulfilled leaders inspire at the deepest levels within an organization.

Shine On

To be a brilliant leader, we need to own our power, influence, and impact. I often see leaders who downplay or minimize their gifts in service of humility. Healthy humility, on the other hand, recognizes that we all are equally human and capable of both greatness and mistakes. From this lens, we see that shining my light only enhances and brightens yours. When we own our power and celebrate our gifts, we enhance the ability for others to do the same. When we shine together, we create even greater access to our full potential. As Shawn Achor writes in his book *Big Potential*, being a top leader doesn't mean you have to be alone. When we can surround ourselves with our constellation of stars, that is when we achieve our greatest potential. He shares, "What you need is a star system: a constellation of positive, authentic influencers who support each other, reinforce each other, and make each other better."

When Brad took over as CEO in January, he stood in front of his organization for the first time in his new role at a company all-hands meeting. Brad decided that the leadership journey we had been on together was something he wanted to share with everyone. He was courageous, transparent, and open about the steps he had gone through to prepare his mind, body, heart, and spirit to take on the CEO role. He shared with everyone the commitments he had made to himself and the culture he wanted to create moving forward. He stood proud to say that leadership and wellbeing would no longer be separate in the company. He wanted an organization and a community where people flourished and reached their greatest potential as whole people. Brad asked for everyone's help in his own journey, to keep him accountable to what he shared on that stage.

I was honored to watch Brad deliver these messages from his heart with such passion and sincerity. I watched the audience connect to Brad deeply and on that day, I watched an entire organization feel inspired. Brad had cultivated more connection and loyalty than he realized. His vulnerability and care were truly moving. After the meeting, Brad and I sat down to debrief. The first thing Brad said to me was, "I can honestly tell you Jamie, I feel fulfillment." I couldn't have been happier to hear those words.

We are most brilliant when we support and shine together. Shine on, Brilliant Leader!

ABOUT THE AUTHOR
JAMIE SHAPIRO

Executive coach, nutritionist, speaker, teacher, and consultant, Jamie Shapiro, CEO of Connected EC, is a leading authority on connecting wellness with leadership performance. A survivor of executive burnout, she understands the incredible pressure executives face in staying connected to both professional and personal goals in demanding environments. Jamie has been coaching and developing high-performing teams since 1998 in executive roles within large-scale corporations.

Through her corporate career, Jamie realized the toll that high-pressure, stressful leadership roles can take. She left the corporate world with a mission to pave a new way for leaders and organizations. Jamie has both an MBA and a Masters in Information Technology and is certified as both an executive coach and a nutritionist. Through her vision, Jamie has brought a new form of holistic coaching to top-level leaders. Jamie's company, Connected EC, helps clients develop a keen awareness of how both their health and mindset have an effect on their capacity to reliably tap into their full leadership capabilities. Jamie bridges the worlds of executive coaching and wellbeing to give people a fresh approach to leadership, enhancing outstanding personal, professional, and organizational performance.

Jamie is also a mother of two wonderful children: Jack who is 10 years old and Ella who is eight years old. She lives in Superior, Colorado, with her loving husband, Sam, and their dog, Diesel.

Additional Resources

Presence: Bringing Your Boldest Self to Your Biggest Challenges by Amy Cuddy. An incredible look at confidence, presence, and the connection to the body.

Work Without Stress: Building a Resilient Mindset for Lasting Success by Derek Roger, PhD and Nick Petrie. A fantastic book on understanding resiliency and stress in the workplace.

Big Potential by Shawn Achor. An exceptional book looking at the impacts of organizational positive psychology on human potential.

Dare to Lead by Brené Brown. A deep look at cultivating heart-centered leadership with vulnerability and trust.

Acknowledgments

First and foremost, I want to thank my supportive, loving, amazing husband, Sam. You are my greatest champion in life and believe in me even when I doubt myself. Without you I could never have followed my dreams to be the woman I am today. Thank you from the bottom of my heart. To my wonderful children, Jack and Ella, you are the lights in my life, my greatest teachers, and my heart. Thank you for giving me the time to create this book. Dad, thank you for always being honest and supporting me unconditionally. Your wisdom is the foundation in everything I do. Your love and belief in me has made this book and everything in my life a reality. Thank you for dedicating your life to making our family flourish. Mom, your love has given me wings. Thank you for teaching me the most important lessons in leadership right from the start. Your patience, kindness, and unconditional love are extraordinary. To my brother, Scott, you continually inspire me. Thank you for always believing in me and supporting my journey. Thank you for being there for me throughout my life on every level. To my Uncle Rick, your friendship, mentorship, and love has been foundational in my life. Thank you. To my entire incredible extended family, thank you for loving and supporting me in all the ways you do. I am so lucky to have such an extraordinary family.

I have had some of the wisest teachers a woman could ask for. Chad, thank you for the generosity, love, and wisdom you have shared with me. I am deeply grateful to have learned from a true master. Your coaching and friendship have been one of the greatest gifts in my life. Thank you. Lauren, our journey together created the ability for me to do my work with extraordinary companies. Thank you for all you have done to make this book a reality. Ben, thank you for being such an incredible teacher and inspiration in embodied leadership. You have believed in this vision right from the start. Catherine, you created the perfect environment and coaching to make this book possible. Thank you for moving my saboteur out of my way and championing my inner author. Victoria, thank you for believing in this book from day one and shining your lovely light on me and this book through your powerful contribution.

I want to also acknowledge the people who have believed in this vision and helped give me a foundation to grow from. JP, Joanne, Anne, JC, Leslie, Rachel, Lynda, Margi, and Melissa, thank you for helping create the perfect support from day one. Without you I would never have been able to build this company. Russell, Steve, and Teresa, thank you for being willing to trust in our journey right from the start. Your unwavering support in connecting the dots of leadership and wellbeing has been deeply inspiring and has given me the ability to grow to where I am today. Julie, thank you for your continued support with this book and in life. Dave, our connection has been one of the greatest gifts I ever received. Thank you for your incredible support. Shawn, your work has inspired me beyond words. Thank you so much for everything. Lindsay, Katie, Tim, Dan, Joshua, Margarita, and Nick, I am beyond grateful for your continued love and friendship. There are truly hundreds of others I could thank. I appreciate the community of brilliant leaders of which I am a part. Thank you to everyone who has reached out a hand to lift me up through the process of creating Connected EC. I am grateful.

Thank You

Thank you so much for taking the time to read *Brilliant*. I hope that the information and tools provided here help you to shine even brighter in your leadership. I would love to keep in touch. Please feel free to sign up for our newsletter and download our free Brilliant Leadership resources at www.connectedec.com.

Made in the USA
Columbia, SC
17 March 2020